PANTRY

**PRESERVING, FREEZING, COOKING AHEAD AND
TASTY MEALS FROM STORECUPBOARD BASICS**

Mrs BEETON'S PANTRY

**PRESERVING, FREEZING, COOKING AHEAD AND
TASTY MEALS FROM STORECUPBOARD BASICS**

Consultant Editor **Bridget Jones**

WARD LOCK

First published 1992 by Ward Lock
Villiers House, 41/47 Strand, London WC2N 5JE

First paperback edition 1993

A Cassell imprint

Designed by Cherry Randell
Edited by Jenni Fleetwood
Photography by Sue Atkinson
Home Economist: Jacqui Hine
Illustrations by Tony Randell

British Library Cataloguing in Publication Data

Beeton, *Mrs, 1836–1865*
  Mrs Beeton's pantry.
  I. Title
  641.5

  ISBN 0-7063-7174-7

Typeset by Best-set Typesetter Ltd., Hong Kong

Printed and bound in Great Britain by Bath Press,
Avon.

Thanks are due to the following for the supply of
furniture and equipment for photography: The Token
House, Peascod Street, Windsor (china); Pine Place,
St Leonard's Road, Windsor, also Henley (pine
tabletop) and The Fireplace Centre, All Saints'
Avenue, Maidenhead, Berks (marble).

CONTENTS

USEFUL WEIGHTS AND MEASURES

USING METRIC OR IMPERIAL MEASURES

Throughout the book, all weights and measures are given first in metric, then in Imperial. For example 100 g/4 oz, 150 ml/¼ pint or 15 ml/ 1 tbsp.

When following any of the recipes use either metric or Imperial – do not combine the two sets of measures as they are not interchangeable.

EQUIVALENT METRIC/IMPERIAL MEASURES

Weights   The following chart lists some of the metric/Imperial weights that are used in the recipes.

METRIC	IMPERIAL
15 g	½ oz
25 g	1 oz
50 g	2 oz
75 g	3 oz
100 g	4 oz
150 g	5 oz
175 g	6 oz
200 g	7 oz
225 g	8 oz
250 g	9 oz
275 g	10 oz
300 g	11 oz
350 g	12 oz
375 g	13 oz
400 g	14 oz
425 g	15 oz
450 g	1 lb
575 g	1¼ lb
675 g	1½ lb
800 g	1¾ lb
900 g	2 lb
1 kg	2¼ lb
1.4 kg	3 lb
1.6 kg	3½ lb
1.8 kg	4 lb
2.25 kg	5 lb

Liquid Measures   The following chart lists some metric/Imperial equivalents for liquids. Millilitres (ml), litres and fluid ounces (fl oz) or pints are used throughout.

METRIC	IMPERIAL
50 ml	2 fl oz
125 ml	4 fl oz
150 ml	¼ pint
300 ml	½ pint
450 ml	¾ pint
600 ml	1 pint

Spoon Measures   Both metric and Imperial equivalents are given for all spoon measures, expressed as millilitres and teaspoons (tsp) or tablespoons (tbsp).

All spoon measures refer to British standard measuring spoons and the quantities given are always for level spoons.

Do not use ordinary kitchen cutlery instead of proper measuring spoons as they will hold quite different quantities.

METRIC	IMPERIAL
1.25 ml	¼ tsp
2.5 ml	½ tsp
5 ml	1 tsp
15 ml	1 tbsp

Length   All linear measures are expressed in millimetres (mm), centimetres (cm) or metres (m) and inches or feet. The following list gives examples of typical conversions.

METRIC	IMPERIAL
5 mm	¼ inch
1 cm	½ inch
2.5 cm	1 inch
5 cm	2 inches
15 cm	6 inches
30 cm	12 inches (1 foot)

OVEN TEMPERATURES

Whenever the oven is used, the required setting is given as three alternatives: degrees Celsius (°C), degrees Fahrenheit (°F) and gas.

The temperature settings given are for conventional ovens. If you have a fan oven, adjust the temperature according to the manufacturer's instructions.

°C	°F	GAS
110	225	¼
120	250	½
140	275	1
150	300	2
160	325	3
180	350	4
190	375	5
200	400	6
220	425	7
230	450	8
240	475	9

MICROWAVE INFORMATION

Occasional microwave hints and instructions are included for certain recipes, as appropriate. The information given is for microwave ovens rated at 650–700 watts.

The following terms have been used for the microwave settings: High, Medium, Defrost and Low. For each setting, the power input is as follows: High = 100% power, Medium = 50% power, Defrost = 30% power and Low = 20% power.

All microwave notes and timings are for guidance only: always read and follow the manufacturer's instructions for your particular appliance. Remember to avoid putting any metal in the microwave and never operate the microwave empty. See also page 13.

NOTES FOR AMERICAN READERS

In America dry goods and liquids are conventionally measured by the standard 8-oz cup. When translating pints, and fractions of pints, Americans should bear in mind that the U.S. pint is equal to 16 fl oz or 2 cups, whereas the Imperial pint is equal to 20 fl oz.

EQUIVALENT METRIC/AMERICAN MEASURES

METRIC/IMPERIAL	AMERICAN
Weights	
450 g/1 lb butter or margarine	2 cups (4 sticks)
100 g/4 oz grated cheese	1 cup
450 g/1 lb flour	4 cups
450 g/1 lb granulated sugar	2 cups
450 g/1 lb icing sugar	3½ cups confectioners' sugar
200 g/7 oz raw long-grain rice	1 cup
100 g/4 oz cooked long-grain rice	1 cup
100 g/4 oz fresh white breadcrumbs	2 cups
Liquid Measures	
150 ml/¼ pint	⅔ cup
300 ml/½ pint	1¼ cups
450 ml/¾ pint	2 cups
600 ml/1 pint	2½ cups
900 ml/1½ pints	3¾ cups
1 litre/1¾ pints	4 cups (2 U.S. pints)

Terminology Some useful American equivalents or substitutes for British ingredients are listed below:

BRITISH	AMERICAN
aubergine	eggplant
bicarbonate of soda	baking soda
biscuits	cookies, crackers
broad beans	fava or lima beans
chicory	endive
cling film	plastic wrap
cornflour	cornstarch
courgettes	zucchini
cream, single	cream, light
cream, double	cream, heavy
flour, plain	flour, all-purpose
frying pan	skillet
grill	broil
minced meat	ground meat
shortcrust pastry	basic pie dough
shrimp	prawn
spring onion	scallion
sultana	golden raisin
swede	rutabaga

INTRODUCTION

This opening chapter briefly outlines the various ways of storing food, with notes on methods to use for different ingredients.

REFRIGERATOR

All fresh, perishable food should be chilled as soon as possible after purchase. The refrigerator should be large enough to store all fresh food bought on regular shopping expeditions and to accommodate extra supplies when these have been bought for one reason or another. For example, if you entertain regularly, your refrigerator should be large enough to cope with the additional food. If the refrigerator is too full, the internal temperature is unlikely to be cold enough.

Temperature Some refrigerators have integral thermometers for checking the running temperature or small thermometers to hang on the shelves are available. The normal running temperature should be 0–3°C/32–37°F. Check the temperature when the refrigerator has been closed for several hours and adjust the controls as necessary.

Food to Refrigerate Dairy produce, such as milk, cheese, butter, eggs and yogurt; margarine and low-fat spreads; fish; meat and all meat products; salad produce and the majority of vegetables; opened canned foods (transferred to a covered container); fruit juices and some drinks; leftover cooked foods and prepared dishes; and any other jars for which chilling is recommended once opened.

Organizing the Refrigerator Warm air rises, so the coldest part of the refrigerator is near the bottom. Highly perishable fresh food, such as fish or meat, should be stored as low as possible, with dairy produce just above. Drinks and cooked dishes may be stored on higher shelves.

Always cover or wrap every item of food. Place raw meat and fish in covered dishes that are large enough to catch any juices. Never let juices from raw foods drip on to other items, particularly cooked food or salad ingredients. If accidental spillage does occur, throw away the affected item.

Defrosting and Cleaning Clean up spills on shelves or bottom of refrigerator at once with hot water and a suitable cleaning agent as recommended by the appliance manufacturer, or use a weak solution of bleach. Follow the manufacturer's instructions for defrosting; many refrigerators do this automatically. Empty the refrigerator occasionally (when stocks are low) and wash it out. Remove all parts as recommended by the manufacturer and ensure that the inside is dry, wiping it with absorbent kitchen paper before replacing food. Do this quickly so that the food stays cool. Use a cool box for short term storage.

FREEZER

The freezer should have an internal temperature of −18°C/0°F. Again, there are a few appliances with integral thermometers but a suitable thermometer is a cheap and useful accessory.

CUPBOARDS

Only non-perishable foods should be stored in a cupboard. Cupboards should be organized according to how cool or warm they are and for ease of access. Flour, sugar, tea, coffee and other frequently used foods should be within easy reach.

Empty cupboards occasionally, wash them out and leave to dry before putting everything back. Rotate stocks to avoid keeping very old ingredients towards the back of a cupboard.

Foods for Cupboard Storage Pasta, rice and cereals; flour, sugar, dried fruit and similar baking ingredients; preserves and pickles; and other foods which have a long shelf life and do not require chilling. Check bought preserves and other foods – although some may be stored in a cupboard until opened, they may require chilling once the seal has been broken.

Pantry or Larder Those who are lucky enough to have a walk-in pantry or larder will find it an invaluable alternative to cool cupboards – ideal for non-perishable foods. However, check that the pantry is dry and cool, not damp, and always use airtight containers for food. Regular cleaning is essential as is occasional redecoration.

Other Storage Areas A cool cellar or utility room is the best place to store potatoes or similar root vegetables. A clean dry cupboard in a utility room or outhouse can be ideal for preserves and pickles.

COOKING FOR AND FROM THE PANTRY

Exploiting food storage facilities to the full makes good sense in terms of time and money. It is sensible to buy in bulk those items you regularly consume, provided you buy large quantities and have the freezer space, to take advantage of reduced prices for multi-buy offers in supermarkets.

Cooking for the storecupboard – and we include the freezer in this definition – means making larger batches of dishes that freeze well – meat sauces, fish cakes, baked items, pancakes and so on – and freezing portions as soon as the food is cool.

This maxim can also be applied to chilling foods. Chilled pâtés, sauces, stuffings and desserts may often be prepared ahead, allowing for excellent meals to be served at short notice. See individual recipes for suggestions on optimum storage times. Some home-made cakes and breads also stay fresh for several days.

Successful Meals in Minutes Keep a stock of versatile canned and dried foods which can be used to create dishes that have both high food value and good flavour. Canned pulses, dried lentils, rice and pasta are typical ingredients. Combined with canned tomatoes, selected canned soups and chilled or vacuum-pack sauces they make life easy on busy days. For the sake of a balanced diet, serve them with simple salads, wholemeal bread, baked potatoes or fresh fruit.

The quality of food cooked from stored ingredients depends on the range of items in stock. Here are a few ideas:

Canned or Frozen Fish Usually excellent, the range includes canned tuna, sardines, kippers, pilchards and salmon. Frozen fish steaks and fillets, prawns, crab meat and whitebait are all examples of versatile ingredients.

Canned fish is quickly transformed into pâtés, can be added to sauces, used to top toast or tossed with rice or pasta.

Frozen or Canned Vegetables Frozen vegetables are, on the whole, a good substitute for fresh but canned vegetables should be chosen with care. Tomatoes, artichoke bottoms, sweetcorn and cream-style corn are all useful, whereas canned peas, carrots and potatoes tend to be significantly inferior in texture (and flavour) compared to frozen or fresh produce.

Sauces, Stocks and Ready-made Items The choice and use depends entirely on individual taste. Quality varies enormously but it is worth looking at all the different types on offer – remember the UHT packs and chilled items as well as canned and dried alternatives. Tomato sauces, plain sauces and custard are all useful; as are good stocks or plain soups (consommé is particularly versatile).

FACTS ABOUT FREEZING

The freezer and frozen food have brought dramatic changes to our eating patterns. Fruit and vegetables are no longer seasonal specialities and, with the refrigerator, the freezer has done away with the need for frequent shopping. Follow the guidelines in this chapter for best results when freezing fresh food, and remember to use all food before the suggested storage time has elapsed.

The choice of freezer depends on where you intend to site it and how you anticipate using it. Measure up, decide on the amount of space available, then thoroughly research all the models on offer before buying. Make a checklist before you shop around, adding features you like as you go.

Chest Freezer Top opening with hinged lid. This is not suitable for a kitchen but is ideal for an unheated garage or utility room. Chest freezers should have a lockable lid to prevent children climbing in; also useful for keeping thieves out if the freezer is in an outhouse or garage. A large amount of food may be packed into a chest freezer but it is not always easy to reach all parts of the appliance, so the contents must be organized for easy access.

Upright Freezer More practical for a kitchen, this type is usually better designed to cope with a warm outside temperature. Also, access is easier. There are some large models of this type but the majority are smaller than chest freezers. Food is more easily organized and accessed in this type of appliance.

Fridge-freezer Generally smaller than an individual appliance (although some very large combination models are available), these are ideal for a kitchen site where the household is small. However, do not forfeit essential refrigerator room in order to gain freezer space.

FOOD TO FREEZE

The freezer can be used in various ways according to your eating and shopping habits and the fruitfulness of your garden. The important point to remember is that the freezer should work for you; you should not change your eating or cooking pattern to fit in with the freezer.

Garden produce, pick-your-own vegetables and fruit, fresh foods and bulk purchases of meat are classic candidates for the freezer. The broad range of ready-frozen foods, sold in large quantities at competitive prices, is also worth exploiting if the products fit in with your eating habits.

Whatever the type of freezer, its position and its use, remember these basic rules.

Temperature The normal running temperature of a freezer should be 0°C/−18°F. When freezing food in bulk, prepare the freezer by turning on fast freeze setting for the advance period indicated in manufacturer's instructions. Leave the fast freeze setting on for the required length of time after putting food in the freezer.

Choice of Food Only freeze food which is in good condition. Do not freeze items that are damaged, bruised or past their prime.

Quantities to Freeze Follow the manufacturer's instructions for the maximum quantity of fresh food to freeze at any one time. This is most important with dense items that take some time to freeze, such as meat.

Packing Food Make sure all food is packed and labelled before putting it in the freezer.

Freezer Record Keep a record of food in the freezer. There are all sorts of complicated ways of doing this, but at the very least you should be aware of what the freezer holds and for roughly how long the food has been frozen. If keeping a freezer diary is not practical, regularly adding or subtracting items as you add or take out a pack, it is important to have regular freezer sort-outs. Bring items that need eating to a prominent position (make a list of goods to be used within the next couple of weeks) and be sure to use them.

Defrosting the Freezer Follow the manufacturer's instructions. Chest freezers should have any ice build-up scraped off with a plastic scraper; they generally need defrosting about once a year. Upright freezers should be defrosted twice a year, or according to the manufacturer's instructions.

PREPARING FOOD FOR FREEZING

All raw food should be prepared as for cooking. Produce should be trimmed, washed and dried. The majority of vegetables should be blanched.

Cooked items should be cooled as quickly as possible, then frozen promptly.

Bought prepared foods or cooked items should be frozen as soon as possible after shopping.

Blanching Vegetables benefit from blanching. Enzymes, naturally present in the food, cause it to ripen, then eventually to become overripe and finally to rot. During freezing, enzyme activity is slowed down considerably but it is not fully halted; in some vegetables therefore, the produce may deteriorate in quality if stored for long periods.

The enzymes are destroyed by exposure to temperatures equal to those of boiling water for a short period of time (this varies according to the food and enzyme). Blanching vegetables destroys the enzymes and improves the keeping quality during freezing.

However, if vegetables are to be frozen for short periods (2–4 weeks), there is no need to blanch them. Some vegetables keep well for far longer periods without blanching; others deteriorate rapidly, developing off flavours. This is particularly true of broad beans, which should always be blanched if storing for longer than 2 weeks.

Blanching Method To prevent food from being cooked during blanching it is important that it is placed in rapidly boiling water, which is brought back to the boil as quickly as possible, then drained immediately. To facilitate speedy cooling, the drained food should be immersed in iced water. This prevents continued cooking by residual heat.

Blanch manageable quantities at a time – if large batches are processed the water takes longer to come back to the boil and the vegetables tend to cook.

Have ready a large saucepan, a wire basket and a large bowl (or thoroughly clean sink) of iced water. Place the prepared vegetables in the basket and plunge them into the boiling water. Bring the water back

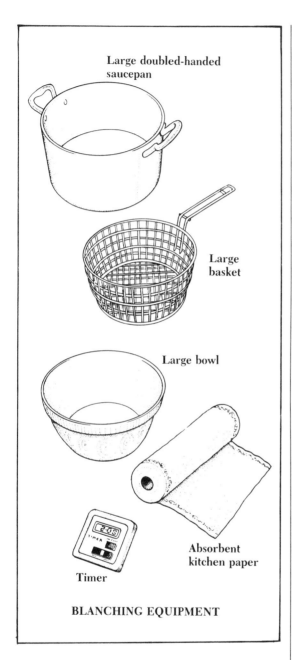

Large doubled-handed saucepan

Large basket

Large bowl

Absorbent kitchen paper

Timer

BLANCHING EQUIPMENT

PACKING FOR FREEZING

To avoid the development of cross-flavours between foods in the freezer and to prevent deterioration in quality, it is essential that all food is adequately packed.

Packing Materials These must be waterproof; they should form an airtight seal when closed. Plastics, whether containers or bags, are ideal. Although foil keeps moisture in, it tends to be too fragile and tears easily.

Sheets of plastic tissue may be used for interleaving stacked items, such as chops or burgers.

Bags should be heavy gauge; thin ones do not keep in moisture, nor do they prevent exposure to the air from causing the food to dry out.

Freezer Burn This results from poor packing: the surface of the food dries out, looks pale and on meat or fish the flesh is slightly shrunken and heavily grained. It is caused by dehydration and is not remedied on thawing and cooking.

Open Freezing This is a useful technique for fish cakes, sausages, strawberries, raspberries and other individual items which are best frozen separately. The food should be prepared, then spread out on trays lined with freezer film or foil. The trays are placed in the freezer until the food is hard, then the items should be packed in airtight bags. This allows large quantities to be packed in one bag, and because the items are free-flowing, small amounts may be removed as required.

Removing Air It is important to remove air from freezer packs as it is a factor in the formation of freezer burn and can cause some fatty foods, such as bacon, to become rancid.

To displace the air, the pack of food may be immersed in a bowl of water. Once all air has been removed, the opening should

to the boil, then time the blanching exactly. Remove the vegetables and plunge them straight into iced water as soon as the required time is reached. Drain well, pat dry on absorbent kitchen paper, then pack and freeze.

be sealed with a wire tie. The exterior of the pack should be dried before freezing.

Labelling Always label packs of food with details of the food or dish, the date and any notes about potential use. For example, note the quantity of sugar added to a fruit purée, if any.

USING FROZEN FOOD

Vegetables should be cooked from frozen. Fruit may also be prepared straight from frozen but the majority of other items should be thawed before use.

Thawing Food The safest way to thaw food is to unwrap it and place it in a covered container in the refrigerator overnight.

The important point to remember is that as the food thaws, the bacteria and enzymes contained in it slowly become active as the temperature rises. While the food remains very cold there is no risk of it being open to contamination by bacterial growth; however if the food is left in a warm room for a long period, parts, if not all, of it will become sufficiently warm for bacteria to grow. Foods left in this manner for long periods may develop high levels of bacteria with the possible consequence of food poisoning.

It is therefore vital that food thawed at room temperature should be frequently monitored. It should be used as soon as it is thawed, while still very cold.

Cooking from Frozen Fish fillets and steaks thaw quickly and may be cooked from frozen; however their texture and flavour is improved if they are thawed first.

Poultry and meat should be thawed before cooking, the only exception being very small or thin items, such as fine strips of meat or poultry, burgers or similar products and thin escalopes. Meat joints may be cooked from frozen but results are not as good as when the meat is thawed. If you must cook from frozen, reduce the cooking

temperature to very low and increase timing to ensure that the centre of the joint is adequately cooked. The drawback with this method is that the outside of the joint may be overcooked or dried out.

Never cook poultry portions or whole poultry from frozen. Poultry may contain bacteria which cause food poisoning and unless the meat is thoroughly cooked these bacteria, or their spores, may survive. Thick areas of poultry should be pierced to check that they are thoroughly cooked; if there is any sign of blood, the poultry should be retured to the oven.

Microwave Thawing The microwave is useful for thawing food. Always read and follow the manufacturer's instructions. As a general guide, use a low or defrost setting. Unpack the frozen food and ensure it is free of metal (for example, clips used to keep poultry limbs in place), then place it in a suitable covered dish. Turn or rearrange items during thawing and observe recommended standing times with larger items to ensure even thawing.

FISH

Only freshly caught or bought fish which has not previously been frozen, then thawed should be frozen. Clean and prepare fish completely and pack in polythene. Separate steaks or fillets with interleaving film.

MEAT, POULTRY AND GAME

Ask the butcher to freeze large quantities of meat, because this would take 3 or 4 days in a home freezer which is not acceptable and would result in poor-quality frozen meat. Smaller quantities of meat, poultry and game can be frozen successfully at home. Meat must be frozen quickly and the fast-freeze switch should be turned on well ahead of freezing time, following the manufacturer's instructions.

Most game must be hung for the required time, then plucked or skinned, and drawn. Surplus fat should be removed, and the meat will take up less space if boned and rolled. Any bones should be padded with a twist of foil or paper before the meat is packed in polythene. Pack chops, steaks, and sausages in small quantities or open freeze them first. Remember that salted meats have a limited storage life since they quickly become rancid.

VEGETABLES

All vegetables should be young, fresh, and clean, and frozen as soon as possible after picking. Open freeze vegetables, then pack them in free-flow packs so that small quantities can be removed as required. Vegetables should be cooked from frozen. Since they are blanched they cook quickly; however the time taken to thaw them means that the overall cooking time is about the same, or slightly less, than for fresh produce. Add the frozen vegetables to boiling water, steam them or toss them in hot butter, according to type.

COOKED AND OTHER PREPARED DISHES

Add rice, pasta or potatoes to liquid dishes after thawing. For long freezer storage, use onions, garlic, herbs and spices with care, as flavours can deteriorate or mature during freezing.

Pack cooked foods in freezer containers, or in ordinary dishes which will withstand freezing and heating. Label carefully if additional ingredients have to be included during re-heating. Use cooked foods within 2 months to retain high quality. Thaw all dishes and make sure they are thoroughly reheated to the original cooking temperature.

CAKES, PASTRY, AND BREADS

Icings and fillings made from fat and sugar are best frozen separately. Fruit or jam fillings in cakes become soggy after thawing, and are better added just before serving. Decorations are also better added then, since they absorb moisture during thawing and may stain the cake. Sweetened whipped cream can be frozen like a cake filling. Pack cakes carefully to avoid crushing during storage. It is better to open freeze decorated cakes before packing.

FRUIT

Freeze only fresh, top-quality fruit. Fruit can be frozen dry and unsweetened, with sugar, in syrup, or as purée, and in cooked dishes. Although the use of sugar or syrup was considered to be important at one time, good results are obtained by freezing fruit without sweetening. Open freezing prevents crushing. Apples discolour; therefore they should be blanched before freezing if not cooked.

FRUIT PURÉE

Prepare purée from raw raspberries or strawberries, but cook other fruit in a little water first. Sweeten to taste before freezing and pack with a little head-space to allow for expansion.

FRUIT JUICES

Prepare fruit juice and freeze in trays. Wrap frozen cubes individually in foil and store in polythene bags. For long storage it is a good idea to bring juice to the boil and to boil it rapidly for a minute, then cool it quickly by standing the pan in iced water.

DAIRY PRODUCE

Most cheeses can be frozen but tend to crumble after being frozen. They should be frozen in small pieces, and cut when still slightly hard. Cream and cottage cheese tends to separate and should not be frozen, although cream cheese can be used for cooking if well beaten after thawing. Only homogenized milk in waxed cartons should be frozen, and then only in small quantities which can be used quickly. Whipped double or whipping cream may be frozen but single cream does not freeze well. Eggs should be very fresh. They should be washed and then broken into a dish to check for quality. They should be frozen already beaten or separated, in rigid containers and sugar or salt added in the proportions shown in the chart on page 21.

FISH AND SHELLFISH FREEZING CHART

Type of fish	Preparation for freezing	High quality storage life	Thawing instructions
Crab, crayfish, and lobster	Cook and cool. Remove flesh before packing. Live crustaceans may be packed in clean polythene carrier bags, then frozen. This is an acceptable method of killing them and they should be cooked from frozen.	1 month (cooked) 3 months (raw)	Thaw in container in refrigerator and serve cold, or add to cooked dishes.
Mussels	Scrub and clean thoroughly. Put in a large pan over medium heat for 3 minutes to open. Cool, remove from shells, and pack in rigid containers with juices or in sauce.	2 months	Cook raw crustaceans as usual, allowing an extra 5 – 10 minutes cooking, depending on size. Thaw in container in refrigerator before adding to dishes.
Oily fish (herring, mackerel, salmon)	Clean well, fillet, cut in steaks or leave whole. Exclude as much air as possible from packs.	2 months	Thaw large fish in refrigerator, but cook small fish from frozen.
Oysters	Open and reserve liquid. Wash in brine (5 ml/1 tsp salt to 500 ml/18 fl oz water). Pack in own liquid.	1 month	Thaw in container in refrigerator and use promptly for cooked dishes.
Prawns and shrimps	Freeze raw or cook and cool in cooking liquid. Remove shells and pack. Shrimps may be covered in melted spiced butter.	1 month	Thaw in container in refrigerator and serve cold, or add to cooked dishes.
Smoked fish	Double pack in polythene bags.	2 months	Thaw in refrigerator to eat cold, or cook haddock and kippers from frozen.
White fish (cod, sole)	Clean, fillet or cut in steaks, or leave whole. Separate pieces of fish with interleaving film. Wrap, excluding air carefully.	3 months	Thaw large fish in refrigerator, but cook small fish from frozen.

MEAT, POULTRY AND GAME FREEZING CHART

Type of meat, poultry, or game	Preparation for freezing	High quality storage life	Thawing instructions
Cubed meat	Pack in small quantities, pressing together tightly.	2–4 months	Thaw in refrigerator for 3–8 hours.
Ham and bacon	Commercial vacuum packs are best. Otherwise, exclude as much air as possible.	2–6 weeks (sliced) 3 months (joints)	Thaw in refrigerator.
Offal	Wash and dry well, remove blood vessels and cores.	1 month	Thaw in refrigerator for 3 hours.
Joints	Trim, bone, and roll, if possible.	9–12 months (beef) 9 months (lamb and veal) 6 months (pork)	Thaw in refrigerator allowing about 4 hours per 450 g/1 lb.
Minced meat	Use lean mince and pack in small quantities.	1 month	Thaw in refrigerator for 3–8 hours.
Sausages and sausagemeat	Pack in small quantities or open freeze.	1 month	Thaw in refrigerator for 3–8 hours.
Steaks, chops or sliced meat	Pack in small quantities or open freeze.	6–12 months (according to meat)	Thaw in refrigerator.
Chicken, guinea-fowl or turkey	Hang, pluck, and draw, if necessary. Truss or cut in joints. Chill for 12 hours. Pack without giblets. Do not stuff.	6–12 months	Thaw in refrigerator.
Giblets	Clean, wash, dry, and chill.	2–4 weeks	Thaw in refrigerator for 2 hours.
Duck and goose	Hang, pluck, and draw, if necessary. Chill for 12 hours. Pack without giblets.	6 months	Thaw in refrigerator. Must be completely thawed before cooking.
Grouse, partridge, pheasant, pigeon	Hang as liked after removing shot and cleaning wounds. Pluck, draw, and truss, and pad bones.	6 months	Thaw in refrigerator.
Plover, quail, snipe, woodcock	Prepare as other game.	6 months	Thaw in refrigerator.
Hares	Clean shot wounds and hang, bleeding the animal and collecting the blood if required. Paunch, skin, clean, and cut into joints. Pack blood separately.	6 months	Thaw in refrigerator.
Rabbits	Paunch, skin, clean, and prepare as for hare.	6 months	Thaw in refrigerator.
Venison	Pack convenient-sized joints. Open freeze steaks, cubes or minced venison.	12 months	Thaw in refrigerator.

VEGETABLE FREEZING CHART

Type of vegetable	Preparation for freezing	Blanching time	High quality storage life
Artichokes (globe)	Remove outer leaves, stalks, and chokes. Add lemon juice to blanching water.	7 minutes	12 months
Artichokes (Jerusalem)	Peel and slice. Cook and purée.	—	3 months
Asparagus	Trim and cut in lengths.	2 minutes (thin) 3 minutes (medium) 4 minutes (large)	9 months
Avocados	Mash pulp with lemon juice (15 ml/1 tbsp juice to each avocado).	—	1 month
Beans (broad)	Shell small young beans.	1½ minutes	12 months
Beans (French)	Top and tail young beans. Leave whole or cut into 2 cm/¾ inch chunks.	3 minutes (whole) 2 minutes (cut)	12 months
Beans (runner)	Cut as preferred.	2 minutes	12 months
Beetroot	Cook very young beet, under 2.5 cm/1 inch in diameter. Peel and leave whole.	—	6 months
Broccoli	Trim stalks and soak in brine for 30 minutes. Wash before blanching.	3 minutes (thin) 4 minutes (medium) 5 minutes (thick)	12 months
Brussels sprouts	Trim and prepare for cooking.	3 minutes (small) 4 minutes (medium)	12 months
Carrots	Use very young carrots. Wash and scrape. Leave whole, dice or slice.	3 minutes	12 months
Cauliflower	Wash and break into florets. Add lemon juice to blanching water.	3 minutes	6 months
Corn on the cob	Use fresh tender corn. Remove husks and silks.	4 minutes (small) 6 minutes (medium) 8 minutes (large)	12 months
Courgettes	Cut courgettes into 1 cm/½ inch slices without peeling.	3 minutes	2 months
Herbs	Wash and pack whole sprigs or chop.	—	6 months
Leeks	Clean and cut into rings.	2 minutes	12 months
Mushrooms	Wipe but do not peel. Pack or open freeze without blanching.	—	3 months
Onions	Skin and chop or slice. Double wrap.	2 minutes	2 months
Parsnips, turnips, and swedes	Peel and dice.	2 minutes	12 months
Peas	Shell young sweet peas.	1 minute	12 months
Peppers	Remove seeds and membranes.	3 minutes (halves) 2 minutes (slices)	12 months
Potatoes	Cook and mash, or make into croquettes. Jacket, baked and roast potatoes can be frozen. Fry chips for 4 minutes but do not brown.	—	3 months
Spinach	Remove any thick stalks and wash leaves very well. Press out moisture after blanching.	2 minutes	12 months
Tomatoes	Purée and pack in rigid cantainers.	—	12 months

COOKED DISHES FREEZING CHART

Type of dish	Preparation for freezing	High quality storage life
Casseroles and stews	Slightly undercook vegetables. Do not add rice, pasta or potatoes. Remove surplus fat.	2 months
Flans (sweet and savoury)	Prepare and bake. Open freeze then wrap.	2 months
Ices – fresh fruit purée	Fully prepare.	3 months
– ice cream	Fully prepare.	3 months
– sorbets and water ices	Fully prepare.	3 months
– bombes and other moulded desserts	Wrap in foil.	3 months
– ice cream gâteaux	Pack in rigid containers or wrap in foil.	3 months
Meat	Do not freeze cooked joints or grilled meats; they can become tough, rancid, and dry. Slice cooked meat thinly and pack in sauce or gravy.	2 months
Meat pies	1) Bake and cool. Wrap. 2) Cook meat filling. Cool and cover with pastry. Wrap.	1) 2 months 2) 2 months
Mousses	Prepare in freezer-tested serving dishes.	1 month
Pancakes	Cool and pack in layers with interleaving film.	2 months
Pasta dishes	Pack pasta and sauce in foil dish with lid.	1 month
Pâté	Cool completely and wrap.	1 month
Pizza	Bake. Cool and wrap. Alternatively, par-bake base, then add topping and freeze.	1 month
Rice	Slightly undercook, drain well, cool, and pack.	1 month
Sauces (savoury)	Prepare completely, but season sparingly. Pack in rigid containers, leaving headspace. *Do not freeze sauces thickened with eggs or cream.*	1 month
Sauces (sweet)	1) Fresh or cooked fruit sauces should be packed in rigid containers, leaving headspace. 2) Thicken pudding sauces with cornflour and pack in rigid containers, leaving headspace. *Do not freeze custard sauces.*	1) 12 months 2) 1 month
Soup	Do not include rice, pasta, barley, potatoes, milk, cream or eggs. Pack in rigid containers, leaving headspace.	2 months
Steamed and baked puddings	Steam or bake puddings in foil containers. Cool and cover.	2 months

BAKED ITEMS FREEZING CHART

Type of cake, pastry or bread	Preparation for freezing	High quality storage life	Thawing/baking instructions
Biscuits	Form dough into 2 cm/¾ inch/ diameter roll. Wrap. **Note** Baked biscuits are best stored in tins without freezing.	2 months	Thaw in refrigerator for 45 minutes. Cut in slices and bake at 190°C/375°F/gas 5, for 10 minutes.
Bread	Pack in polythene bags. Crusty bread quickly loses its crispness in the freezer.	1 month	Thaw at room temperature for 4 hours.
Breadcrumbs (plain)	Pack in polythene bags.	3 months	Use from frozen.
Brioches and croissants	Pack in rigid containers to prevent crushing, immediately after baking and cooling.	1 month	Thaw at room temperature for 30 minutes and heat in oven or under grill.
Cakes (uniced)	Cool completely and wrap.	4 months	Thaw at room temperature for 2–3 hours.
Cheesecakes	Make baked or refrigerated variety in cake tin with removable base. Open freeze and pack in rigid container. Types relying on gelatine for texture and shape are best avoided as they become very soft on thawing.	1 month	Thaw for 8 hours in refrigerator.
Choux pastries	Bake but do not fill or ice. Pack in polythene bags or boxes.	1 month	Thaw at room temperature for 2 hours. Crisp for a minute in the oven.
Crumpets and muffins	Pack in polythene bags.	1 month	Thaw in wrappings at room temperature for 30 minutes before toasting.
Danish pastries	Bake but do not ice. Pack in foil trays with lids, or in rigid containers.	2 months	Thaw at room temperature for 1 hour. Heat if liked.
Fruit pies	Brush bottom crust with egg white to prevent sogginess: 1) Bake, cool, and pack. 2) Use uncooked fruit and pastry, open freeze, and pack.	1) 4 months 2) 2 months	1) Thaw to serve cold, or reheat. 2) Bake from frozen at 200°C/ 400°F/gas 6 for 1 hour.
Pastry cases	Freeze baked or unbaked, using foil containers.	4 months	Bake frozen cases at recommended temperatures for type of pastry. Re-heat baked cases, or fill with hot filling.
Sandwiches	Do not remove crusts. Spread with butter or margarine. Do not use salad fillings, mayonnaise or hard-boiled eggs. Separate sandwiches with interleaving film and pack in foil or polythene. Cheese, diced chicken with soft cheese, diced ham and grated cheese or mashed sardines are examples of suitable fillings.	1 month	Thaw at room temperature and remove crusts, or toast under grill while still frozen.
Scones	Pack in small quantities.	2 months	Thaw at room temperature for 1 hour. Alternatively, bake frozen scones at 180°C/350°F/ gas 4 for 10 minutes.

FRUIT FREEZING CHART

Type of fruit	Preparation for freezing	High quality storage life
Apples	Peel, core, and slice. Blanch in boiling water with lemon juice added for 1 minute.	12 months
Apricots	Skin and cut in halves or slices. Add lemon juice to pack.	12 months
Blackberries and raspberries	Clean and hull.	12 months
Blueberries	Wash and drain. Crush slightly to soften skins.	12 months
Cherries	Chill in water for 1 hour and stone.	12 months
Cranberries	Wash and drain.	12 months
Currants (red, white, and black)	Strip fruit from stems.	12 months
Damsons	Wash, drain, and stone.	12 months
Gooseberries	Clean, top, and tail.	12 months
Greengages and plums	Cut in half and stone.	12 months
Lemons and limes	Peel and slice, or slice without peeling and pack for drinks.	12 months
Peaches and nectarines	Skin, cut in halves or slices, and brush with lemon juice. Alternatively, make a raw purée with 15 ml/ 1 tbsp lemon juice to 450 g/1 lb fruit.	12 months
Pineapple	Peel and cut in slices or chunks.	12 months
Rhubarb	Wash in cold water and trim sticks.	12 months
Strawberries	Clean and grade for size.	12 months

DAIRY PRODUCE FREEZING CHART

Dairy produce	Preparation for freezing	High quality storage life	Thawing instructions
Butter and margarine	Overwrap in foil or polythene.	6 months (unsalted) 3 months (salted)	Thaw enough for 1 week's use in refrigerator.
Cheese – hard	Cut in 200 g/7 oz pieces and wrap in foil or polythene. Pack grated cheese in polythene bags. Double wrap blue cheeses.	3 months	Thaw in open wrappings at room temperature for 3 hours. Cut while slightly frozen to avoid crumbling.
– cream	Blend with double cream.	3 months	Thaw in container in refrigerator overnight. Blend with fork to restore smoothness.
Cream	Freeze all creams in cartons. Do not freeze single, soured or half-cream.	6 months	Thaw in carton at room temperature and stir with a fork to restore smoothness.
– whipped	Sweeten with 30 ml/2 tbsp sugar to 600 ml/1 pint cream. Freeze in containers, or open freeze piped rosettes.	6 months	Thaw in container at room temperature. Rosettes thaw in 15 minutes at room temperature.
Eggs	*Do not freeze in shell.* 1) Mix yolks and whites, adding 5 ml/1 tsp salt or 10 ml/2 tsp sugar to 5 eggs. 2) Mix yolks, adding 5 ml/1 tsp salt or 10 ml/2 tsp sugar to 5 yolks. 3) Put whites in containers with no addition.	12 months	Thaw in refrigerator but bring to room temperature before use.
Milk	Only homogenized milk can be frozen. Leave 2 cm/¾ inch headspace.	1 month	Thaw at room temperature and use quickly.

PATES AND POTTED FOODS

Home-made pâtés and potted foods have a character of their own, quite different from bought types and definitely superior to the majority of commercial preparations. With careful preparation, prompt cooling and chilling, they keep well in the refrigerator – ideal for impressing weekend guests, for picnics or holiday meals.

A pâté is a coarse or fine mixture, seasoned and flavoured for serving cold. Fish, meat, offal, poultry, game, cheese, vegetables or pulses may be potted or used to make pâtés; this chapter includes a selection of popular recipes.

PREPARATION TECHNIQUES

Mincing or Puréeing When this is carried out, depends on the recipe. Some pâtés require the raw meat, offal, onions and bread to be processed until smooth, then combined and cooked. Other recipes par-cook the meat or offal before processing. Potted foods are usually cooked, if necessary, before being puréed.

A mincer is the best appliance for puréeing raw meat, whereas a food processor or blender may be used for par-cooked or cooked meat. Use a coarse blade first, followed by a fine one. For a very smooth result, the purée may be sieved.

Stretching Bacon for Lining Some pâtés are cooked in a tin, terrine or dish which is first lined with bacon rashers. Streaky bacon should be used and the rashers should be stretched with the back of a knife. When they are thin and long, lay them in the dish, overlapping each rasher and leaving extra length overhanging the edge. When the dish is filled with pâté, the ends of the bacon should be folded over the top of the mixture.

Baking in a Bain Marie To prevent the outside of the pâté from overcooking before the centre has cooked, the dish or container is placed in a roasting tin. Hot water is poured into the roasting tin to just below its rim, and the pâté is then baked. The water should be topped up during cooking.

Weighting To give the pâté its charac-teristic dense texture it should be weighted after cooking. Cover the top of the pâté with greaseproof paper and foil, then place a heavy weight on top. If the pâté has been cooked in a round dish, place a plate on top before adding the weight; the plate should be slightly smaller in diameter than the dish. Leave the pâté until cold, then chill overnight.

Cans of food, scale weights or other suitable heavy items may be used to weight the pâté. Remember to stand the dish in an outer container to catch any juices that spill over from the pâté.

Storage and Usage Always keep pâtés and potted foods covered on a low shelf in the refrigerator. Remove slices or portions as required and return the rest to the refrigerator promptly. Most pâtés improve if they are allowed to mature for 1–2 days, but they should be eaten within a week. Pâtés made from poultry livers are the exception; they should be made and eaten within 2 days. Always use perfectly fresh ingredients for making pâtés and follow recipes with care.

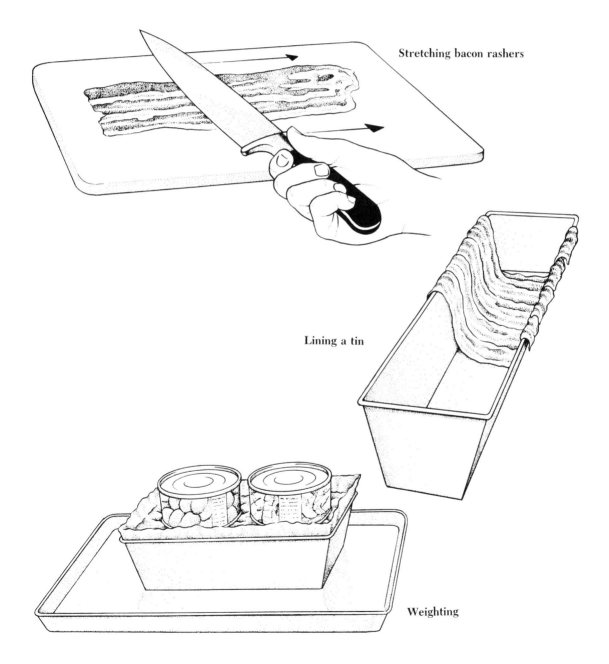

Stretching bacon rashers

Lining a tin

Weighting

LIVER PATE

Serve this flavoursome pâté in the dish in which it was cooked, with hot dry toast, or cut into slices and serve with salad.

fat for greasing
75 g/3 oz butter
100 g/4 oz lean rindless bacon rashers, chopped
225 g/8 oz calf's or pig's liver, trimmed and chopped
225 g/8 oz chicken livers, trimmed and chopped
1 small onion, finely chopped
a few gherkins, chopped (optional)
1–2 hard-boiled eggs, chopped
salt and pepper
5–10 ml/1–2 tsp dried mixed herbs
clarified butter, melted (see Mrs Beeton's Tip)

Grease an ovenproof terrine or similar dish. Set the oven at 180°C/350°F/gas 4. Melt the butter in a frying pan, add the bacon, livers and onion and fry gently for 5–6 minutes. Mince finely twice or process in a blender or food processor to a smooth paste.

Add the chopped gherkins and hard-boiled eggs, with salt, pepper and herbs to taste. Stir well. Spoon into the prepared dish and cover with buttered greaseproof paper.

Stand the dish in a roasting tin and add enough hot water to come to within 2.5 cm/1 inch of the rim of the tin. Bake for 30 minutes.

When cooked, cover immediately with a layer of clarified butter. Leave to cool, then chill before serving. Alternatively, place under a light weight (see Mrs Beeton's Tip opposite) and cover with clarified butter when cold.

MAKES ABOUT 675 G/1½ LB

> 🥄 **MRS BEETON'S TIP** To clarify butter, heat gently until melted, then stand for 2–3 minutes. Carefully pour the clear yellow liquid on top into a clean bowl, leaving the residue behind. This is the clarified butter.

───────── ◈ ─────────

PATE MAISON

Illustrated on page 33

8–10 rindless back bacon rashers
100 g/4 oz pig's liver, trimmed and coarsely chopped
100 g/4 oz rindless boned belly of pork, coarsely chopped
225 g/8 oz sausagemeat
225 g/8 oz cold cooked rabbit, finely chopped
1 onion, finely chopped
25 g/1 oz soft white breadcrumbs
1 egg, beaten
15 ml/1 tbsp milk
75 ml/3 fl oz brandy
salt and pepper
3 bay leaves to garnish

Set the oven at 180°C/350°F/gas 4. Arrange the bay leaves on the base of a

1.25 litre/2¼ pint rectangular ovenproof dish or terrine. Lay the bacon rashers flat on a board, one at a time, and stretch them with the back of a knife until quite thin. Set aside two or three rashers for the topping and use the rest to line the dish, overlapping them neatly.

Combine the chopped liver, pork, sausagemeat, rabbit, onion and breadcrumbs in a mixing bowl. Stir in the egg, milk and brandy, with salt and pepper to taste.

Spoon the mixture into the lined dish, cover with the reserved bacon rashers and then with a lid or foil. Stand the dish in a roasting tin and add enough hot water to come to within 2.5 cm/1 inch of the rim of the tin.

When cooked, weight the pâté (see Mrs Beeton's Tip) and leave to cool. Chill for 18–24 hours. To serve, remove the top bacon rashers and invert the pâté on a platter.

MAKES ABOUT 1 KG/2¼ LB

🥣MRS BEETON'S TIP To weight a pâté, cut a piece of stout card to fit the top of the dish, cover it with foil and place lightly on top of the pâté. Add a light weight such as a can of fruit and cool the pâté by standing the dish in a pan of iced water which comes halfway up its sides. When cold, remove any fat from the sides, cover with clarified butter (if liked) and chill before serving. If a dense pâté is required, the light weight may be replaced with a heavier one once the pâté is cool.

RABBIT TERRINE

2 oven-ready pigeons
1(1 kg/2¼ lb) rabbit, skinned and boned
    or 450 g/1 lb boneless rabbit meat
100 g/4 oz pig's liver, trimmed and sliced
150 ml/¼ pint red wine
1 bay leaf
275 g/10 oz unsmoked rindless streaky
    bacon rashers
450 g/1 lb rindless boned belly of pork,
    coarsely chopped
1 garlic clove, crushed
30 ml/2 tbsp brandy
freshly ground black pepper

Remove the pigeon meat from the bones and place in a mixing bowl with the rabbit meat. Add the liver, wine and bay leaf. Cover tightly and marinate overnight in the refrigerator.

Stretch the bacon rashers lightly with the back of a knife and line a 2 litre/3½ pint terrine or pie dish. Set the oven at 160°C/325°F/gas 3.

Drain the meat, reserving the marinade. Mince the pork and marinated meats or process roughly in a food processor. Stir in the garlic, reserved marinade and brandy. Season with plenty of black pepper.

Spoon the mixture into the prepared terrine and cover with foil or a lid. Stand the dish in a roasting tin and add enough hot water to come to within 2.5 cm/1 inch of the rim of the tin. Bake for about 2 hours.

When cooked, pour off any excess liquid and weight the pâté (see Mrs Beeton's Tip left). Cool, then chill before serving.

MAKES ABOUT 1.6 KG/3½ LB

POTTED HAM

Illustrated on page 33

butter for greasing
1.25 kg/2¾ lb cooked ham, not too lean
1.25 ml/¼ tsp ground mace
1.25 ml/¼ tsp grated nutmeg
pinch of cayenne pepper
1.25 ml/¼ tsp ground black pepper
melted clarified butter (see Mrs Beeton's
    Tip, page 24)

Grease a pie dish. Set the oven at 180°C/350°F/gas 4. Mince the ham two or three times, then pound well and rub through a fine sieve into a clean bowl. Add the spices and peppers and mix well. Spoon the ham mixture into the prepared dish, cover with buttered greaseproof paper and bake for about 45 minutes.

When cooked, allow to cool, then turn into small pots and cover with clarified butter. Refrigerate until the butter is firm.

MAKES ABOUT 1 KG/2¼ LB

POTTED VENISON

100–150 g/4–5 oz butter
1 kg/2¼ lb cooked venison, finely minced
60 ml/4 tbsp port or brown stock
1.25 ml/¼ tsp grated nutmeg
1.25 ml/¼ tsp ground allspice
salt
2.5 ml/½ tsp freshly ground black pepper
melted clarified butter (see Mrs Beeton's
    Tip, page 24)

Melt 100 g/4 oz of the butter in a saucepan. Add the minced venison, port or stock, spices, salt and pepper. If the meat is very dry, add the remaining butter.

Cook the mixture gently until blended and thoroughly hot. Immediately, turn into small pots and leave to cool. Cover with clarified butter. When cool, refrigerate until the butter is firm.

MAKES ABOUT 1 KG/2¼ LB

POTTED BEEF

A popular Victorian dish, potted beef will keep for up to a week in the refrigerator when made from very fresh meat and sealed with clarified butter. Chuck and skirt steak are both ideal cuts to use.

butter for greasing
450 g/1 lb lean braising steak, trimmed
    and cubed
blade of mace
pinch of ground ginger
30 ml/2 tbsp beef stock
75 g/3 oz butter
salt and pepper
melted clarified butter (see Mrs Beeton's
    Tip, page 24)

Set the oven at 150°C/300°F/gas 2. Combine the beef cubes, mace, ginger and stock in a casserole or ovenproof dish. Cover tightly with buttered greaseproof paper and foil.

Bake for 3½–4 hours, until the meat is very tender. Remove the mace. Mince the meat twice, then pound it well with the butter and any meat juices remaining in the casserole to make a smooth paste. Add salt and pepper to taste.

Turn into small pots and cover with clarified butter. When cool, refrigerate until the butter is firm.

MAKES ABOUT 450 G/1 LB

POTTED MUSHROOMS

Illustrated on page 33

450 g/1 lb mushrooms, finely chopped
50 g/2 oz butter
salt and pepper
pinch of ground allspice
2 anchovy fillets, mashed finely
melted clarified butter (see Mrs Beeton's
    Tip, page 24)

Place the mushrooms in a heavy bottomed saucepan over gentle heat until the juice runs freely. Raise the heat and cook, uncovered, stirring often until all the juice evaporates and the mushrooms are dry.

Add the butter with salt and pepper to taste. Sprinkle with the allspice and continue cooking for about 5 minutes, or until all the butter is absorbed.

Stir in the anchovies and cook for 2 minutes more. Remove from the heat, turn into small pots and leave to cool. Cover with clarified butter. Refrigerate until the butter is firm, then add a second layer of clarified butter. Use within 5 days.

MAKES ABOUT 300 G/11 OZ

> **MRS BEETON'S TIP** Mushrooms should be used within three days of purchase. The best way to store loose mushrooms is in a clean paper bag inside a plastic bag or box. The plastic container will conserve moisture while the paper absorbs any condensation. Store in the bottom of the refrigerator.

POTTED CHEESE

450 g/1 lb mature Cheddar or Cheshire
    cheese, finely grated
100 g/4 oz butter, softened
salt
pinch of ground mace
50–75 ml/2–3 fl oz cream sherry or
    tawny port
melted clarified butter (see Mrs Beeton's
    Tip, page 24), (optional)

Pound about one third of the cheese with the butter until smooth, or process in a blender or food processor. Add the remaining cheese, with the salt, mace and sherry or port. Pound to a smooth paste.

Turn into small pots. Cover with clarified butter. When cool, refrigerate until the butter is firm. Alternatively, cover with waxed paper, or greaseproof paper and cling film before refrigerating.

MAKES ABOUT 450 G/1 LB

VARIATION

POTTED STILTON Make as above. Use tawny or ruby port to moisten but add with discretion. A good Stilton should need very little.

> **MRS BEETON'S TIP** Potted cheese makes a marvellous filling for celery savouries. Carefully dismantle a perfect head of crisp celery. Wash and dry the sticks, then, starting with an inner stick, spread it liberally with potted cheese. Reassemble the head of celery, using the potted cheese as 'cement' for the sticks. When the head is assembled, press the sticks firmly together, wrap in greaseproof paper and refrigerate for 1–2 hours. Slice and serve on crackers or slices of bread.

DAIRY PRODUCE

This short section includes a few traditional techniques often overlooked today – like making soft cheese or junket. Both are easy to prepare and excellent to eat; versatile ingredients for savouries, the cheeseboard or desserts. Basic instructions, plus additional dairy recipes are in the pages that follow.

When preparing any food that requires long standing, straining or fermentation, always make sure that all ingredients are absolutely fresh and equipment is scrupulously clean. Do not try to rush the process of straining curds or fermenting yogurt; equally, do not leave the food in a warm place, or without covering and chilling, for any length of time after the process is complete.

EQUIPMENT

You do not need a stack of specialist equipment to make soft cheese or yogurt. The instructions for making yogurt outline the process clearly; although a yogurt maker is useful, a vacuum flask serves just as well.

For straining curds you will need a fine muslin cloth, some form of stand or a fine sieve and large bowl.

A thermometer is useful to check the temperature of milk but it is not essential; most sugar thermometers will serve the purpose well enough.

All equipment should be thoroughly cleaned, then scalded in boiling water for 5 minutes before use.

TECHNIQUES

Hanging or Straining Since few modern homes have a cold room with marble slab and convenient hook above, hanging curds to separate them from the whey may mean devising a special contraption.

A jelly bag and stand for preserving is ideal. If this is not available, use a pair of metal coat hangers, slotted together and bound in place with wire. The jelly bag or cloth may be hung from the four corners.

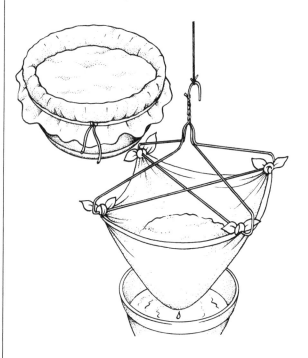

Alternatively, if you have a very large mixing bowl with a rim, a length of muslin may be secured loosely over it with elastic. Tie the length of elastic first, then slip it over the edge of the bowl so that it fits under the rim when the muslin is in place.

Squeezing Whey To reduce the amount of moisture in curds, gather up the muslin and squeeze out extra whey by twisting ends of the fabric. Take care not to squeeze too hard as this may cause the soft cheese to be pressed through the muslin.

Weighting The curds may be placed in a dish and weighted to give a closer-textured cheese. Line a suitable dish or container with scalded muslin, then spoon in the curds and press them down. Cover with more muslin, or fold over the ends, and weight the cheese with a heavy object wrapped in polythene. Stand the dish in a container. Chill overnight, then remove the weight and turn out the cheese.

*H*OME-MADE YOGURT

Yogurt can easily be made at home. It will not always have the consistency of the commercial product, but the results will be successful if a few simple rules are followed. The yogurt will keep for 4–5 days in a refrigerator. A new carton of commercial yogurt will be needed for the next incubation.

The yogurt can be incubated in one of three ways:

■ In an electric, thermostatically controlled incubator. These are very useful if the family eats a lot of yogurt.

■ In a wide-necked vacuum flask (a narrow-necked flask is not suitable as the yogurt is broken up when it is removed). This is suitable for smaller quantities of yogurt.

■ In a home-made incubator made from a large biscuit or cake tin with a lid. Line the base and sides with an insulating material such as woollen fabric or cotton wool and have a piece of material large enough to fit inside the top. Use 4 or 5 screw-topped glass jars that will fit inside the incubator.

METHOD

■ Sterilize all equipment to be used by immersion in boiling water for at least 3 minutes or by using a commercial sterilizing solution.

■ Heat 500 ml/17 fl oz UHT or sterilized milk to 43°C/108°F in a saucepan (use a cooking thermometer) and blend in 5 ml/1 tsp *fresh* natural yogurt. Alternatively use a yogurt starter culture (obtainable with full instructions from dairy laboratories).

■ Pour into pots or glasses, if using. Place in the prepared incubator, seal, and leave for 6–8 hours.

■ Turn the yogurt into a cold bowl and cool rapidly, standing the bowl in cold water and whisking the yogurt until creamy.

■ Cover the bowl and chill for about 4 hours when the yogurt will have thickened further.

■ When serving, gently stir in sugar. Flavour with stewed fruit or jam.

☀ **MICROWAVE TIP** Yogurt can be made in the microwave. Heat 600 ml/1 pint milk in a large bowl on High for 6 minutes. Cool until tepid (about 46°C/115°F) and stir in 15 ml/1 tbsp plain yogurt. Add 30 ml/2 tbsp dried full-cream powdered milk. Beat well. Cover the bowl and heat on Low for 70 minutes. Cool, then chill until required.

USING YOGURTS IN PUDDINGS

■ Substitute plain yogurt for cream to give a lighter texture and sharper flavour in cold desserts.

■ Spread a thick layer of plain yogurt or Greek yogurt over drained canned apricots in a shallow gratin dish. Top with a generous coating of brown sugar and flash under a hot grill to make a wonderful fruit brûlée.

■ Stir clear honey into plain yogurt. Add toasted almonds just before serving.

■ Make a tangy fruit jelly by dissolving a jelly tablet in a half quantity of hot water. Allow the jelly to cool before stirring it into an equal quantity of plain yogurt. Pour into a mould or individual dishes and chill until set.

SOFT CHEESE

The perfect way to use up excess milk, soft cheese can be flavoured with finely chopped herbs, ground or crushed whole spices or finely drained chopped fruit. The quantity of flavouring used will vary, but as a general rule, 1.25 ml/¼ tsp crushed spice or 5 ml/1 tsp solid flavouring is sufficient for 200 g/7 oz cheese. Pay particular attention to hygiene when making soft cheese; ensure all equipment is scrupulously clean and hang the cheese in a cold place.

2.6 litres/4½ pints fresh or slightly soured milk
20 ml/4 tsp rennet essence
salt
30–60 ml/2–4 tbsp single cream

Warm the milk gently (30–35°C/ 86–95°F) and pour into a bowl. Stir in the rennet essence and leave to stand at room temperature until a curd forms. Meanwhile, line a metal sieve with a scalded piece of muslin about 25 cm/10 inches square. Stand the sieve over a bowl.

Gently tip the curdled milk into the cloth, bring the corners of the cloth up and tie securely with string. Hang above the bowl to catch the dripping whey. Leave for 6–8 hours; longer if a fairly thick cloth is used.

Open the bag and scrape down any curd on the sides of the cloth to form one mass. Cut any solid curd into small pieces. Tie the bag up again, hang it up and continue draining. Repeat the scraping down and cutting once or twice more until the cheese reaches the required consistency. This can be judged by squeezing the bag gently.

Turn the curd into a bowl. Mix in salt to taste gently but thoroughly. Blend in cream and add any flavouring used (see Mrs Beeton's Tip). Form the cheese into pats or turn into pots or cartons. Cover and chill until required. Use within 36 hours; 24 hours if flavoured with solid fresh flavouring such as herbs.

MAKES ABOUT 500 G/18 OZ

MRS BEETON'S TIP If the cheese is softer than desired once flavouring has been added, return it to the bag and allow to drain again for 3–6 hours.

SIMPLE SOFT CHEESE

Strictly speaking this is not a cheese at all – it is strained yogurt which becomes thick and similar in texture to a soft cheese. It can be used in place of soft cheese in many recipes or flavoured to serve as a spread.

30 ml/2 tbsp lemon juice
1.1 litres/2 pints yogurt or low-fat
　　fromage frais

Have ready a large piece of double-thick scalded muslin. Put the yogurt or fromage frais in a bowl and stir in the lemon juice. Pour the mixture into the muslin and gather up the corners, then hang the yogurt or fromage frais overnight in a cool place.

Discard the liquid, then use a spatula to scrape the 'cheese' into a bowl. Cover and chill until ready for use.

MAKES ABOUT 225 G/8 OZ

VARIATIONS

■ Add salt and pepper to taste. Mix in chopped parsley, a little chopped fresh tarragon, some chopped thyme and a little crushed garlic (if liked). Press neatly into a dish and chill until ready to serve with crackers or crusty bread.

■ Mix 50 g/2 oz finely chopped walnuts and 45 ml/3 tbsp snipped chives into the cheese.

■ Finely chop ½ seeded red pepper, then add it to the cheese with 30 ml/ 2 tbsp grated onion and salt and pepper to taste.

■ Make a sweet cheese by adding grated orange rind and sugar to taste.

JUNKET

The type of milk and the temperature are very important in the making of junket. The milk must not be sterilized nor must it be UHT milk, and it must be at the correct temperature; if it is too hot or too cold, it will not set. The junket should be left to set in a warm room; it should not be put in a refrigerator.

600 ml/l pint milk
15 ml/l tbsp sugar
few drops of vanilla essence
5 ml/l tsp rennet essence
grated nutmeg or ground cinnamon

In a saucepan, warm the milk to blood-heat (about 37°C/98°F) with the sugar and vanilla essence. Stir in the rennet essence.

Pour the mixture into 1 large or 4 small dishes. Cover and leave to stand in a warm place for about 1 hour or until set. Do not move the junket at this stage.

Sprinkle the junket with spice and serve cold but not chilled.

SERVES 4

VARIATIONS

ALMOND OR RUM JUNKET Instead of the vanilla essence, add 2.5 ml/½ tsp almond or rum essence to the milk. Decorate with toasted almonds, if liked.
LEMON OR ORANGE JUNKET Infuse the pared rind of 1 lemon or orange in the milk. Using a few drops of food colouring, tint the junket pale yellow or orange. Do not use any other flavouring.
RICH JUNKET Run a layer of single cream, flavoured with brandy, if liked, over the top of the junket. Flavour in any of the ways given above.

WELSH RAREBIT

The cheese paste will keep in the refrigerator for up to 5 days, ready for spreading on toast and grilling.

25 g/l oz butter
15 ml/l tbsp plain flour
75 ml/5 tbsp milk or 30 ml/2 tbsp milk and
    45 ml/3 tbsp ale or beer
5 ml/l tsp French mustard
few drops of Worcestershire sauce (see
    page 137)
175 g/6 oz Cheddar cheese, grated
salt and pepper

Melt the butter in a saucepan, stir in the flour and cook over gentle heat for 2–3 minutes, stirring constantly. Do not let the flour colour. Stir in the milk and blend to a smooth, thick mixture, then stir in the ale or beer, if used. Add the mustard and Worcestershire sauce.

Gradually add the cheese, stirring after each addition. Remove from the heat as soon as the mixture is smooth. Add salt and pepper to taste. Place in a covered container and chill when cool.

To use the rarebit, spread the mixture on buttered toast and place under a preheated hot grill for 2–3 minutes until bubbling and lightly browned. Serve at once.

SERVES 4 TO 6

VARIATIONS

BUCK RAREBIT Make as for Welsh Rarebit, but top each slice with a poached egg.
YORKSHIRE RAREBIT Make as for Welsh Rarebit, but add 4 grilled rindless back bacon rashers.

IRISH RAREBIT

100 g/4 oz mild Cheddar cheese, grated
60 ml/4 tbsp milk
25 g/l oz butter
5 ml/l tsp mild white vinegar
5 ml/l tsp prepared English mustard
salt and pepper
10 ml/2 tsp chopped gherkin

Combine the cheese, milk and butter in a saucepan. Cook over gentle heat, stirring constantly, until the cheese has melted and the mixture is smooth and creamy. Stir in the vinegar and mustard, with salt and pepper to taste. Add the gherkin. Transfer to a container, cover and chill when cold.

To use the rarebit, spread the mixture on buttered toast and grill briefly under moderate heat to brown the surface.

SERVES 2

CURRY CHEESE TOPPER

15 ml/l tbsp apricot or mango chutney
100 g/4 oz mature Cheddar cheese,
    grated
5 ml/l tsp curry powder

Chop any large chunks in the chutney. Pound the cheese, chutney and curry powder together in a small bowl. Place the mixture in a covered container in the refrigerator until ready for use.

To use the mixture, spread it on buttered toast and grill for 3–4 minutes until browned or serve on plain crackers.

SERVES 2

From the top: Pâté Maison (page 24), Potted Mushrooms (page 27) and Potted Ham (page 26)

Coeur à la Crème au Citron (page 37)

Mixed Fruit Loaf and Cherry Cake (both on page 41)

From the middle of the basket, outwards: **Caraway Crackers (page 44), Oatcakes (page 45) and Crisp Crackers (page 43)**

COEUR A LA CREME AU CITRON

Illustrated on page 34

150 ml/¼ pint double cream
pinch of salt
150 g/5 oz low-fat curd cheese
50 g/2 oz caster sugar
grated rind and juice of 1 lemon
2 egg whites

Line a 400 ml/14 fl oz heart-shaped coeur à la crème mould with greaseproof paper. In a bowl whip the cream with the salt until it holds soft peaks. Break up the curd cheese with a fork, and whisk it gradually into the cream with the sugar. Do not let the mixture lose stiffness.

Fold the lemon rind and juice into the cream as lightly as possible.

In a clean, grease-free bowl, whisk the egg whites until they hold stiff peaks. Fold them into the mixture, then very gently turn the mixture into the mould, filling all the corners.

Stand the mould in a large dish or roasting tin to catch the liquid which seeps from the mixture. Chill for at least 2 hours or overnight. Turn out and serve with single cream.

SERVES 6

🥣 MRS BEETON'S TIP Individual coeur à la crème moulds may be used. If these are unavailable, clean yogurt pots, with several drainage holes punched in the base of each, make an acceptable substitute.

BAKED LEMON CHEESECAKE

BASE
50 g/2 oz butter or margarine
50 g/2 oz caster sugar
1 egg, beaten
50 g/2 oz self-raising flour
2.5 ml/½ tsp baking powder

FILLING
75 g/3 oz butter
100 g/4 oz caster sugar
grated rind of 1 lemon
15 ml/1 tbsp lemon juice
2 eggs
50 g/2 oz plain flour
75 g/3 oz sultanas
450 g/1 lb full-fat soft cheese
250 ml/8 fl oz double cream

Set the oven at 160°C/325°F/gas 3. Make the base. Combine all the ingredients in a mixing bowl and beat until smooth. Spread the mixture over the base of a deep loose-bottomed 20 cm/8 in round cake tin.

For the filling, cream the butter with the sugar in a large bowl until light and fluffy. Stir in the lemon rind and juice. Add the eggs one at a time, beating after each addition and adding a little flour, if necessary, to stabilize the mixture. Fold in the remaining flour and sultanas.

In a separate bowl, beat the cheese until smooth. Gradually beat in the cream. Fold the cheese mixture carefully into the butter mixture and spoon into the prepared tin.

Bake for 1¼–1½ hours or until firm. Cool, then remove from the tin and transfer to a serving plate. Serve cold.

SERVES 10 TO 12

BREADS, CAKES AND BISCUITS

Home-made breads, cakes and biscuits make pleasing and practical pantry goods, whether baked once a week or in occasional batches for freezing. In addition to sweet favourites, remember that crackers, oatcakes and other savoury biscuits are easy to prepare and taste splendid with cheese and fruit for supper or a light meal.

The storage life for baked items varies according to type. On the whole, home-made bread does not keep as well as its commercial equivalent but it may be frozen when freshly made and cooled. Home-made muffins and crumpets are just as easy to make in large batches as a few at a time, so it makes good sense to freeze them.

The keeping quality of biscuits, like that of bread, varies. Most bought varieties keep for many months in unopened packets. Home-baked biscuits will keep for several weeks in a sealed polythene bag in an airtight container in a cool place. They can be frozen cooked, but it is far more satisfactory to freeze the prepared dough, either shaped into rounds and ready to bake or in a ready-to-slice roll. To bake a small batch of biscuits, allow the frozen roll of dough to stand in the refrigerator for 15 minutes, cut off neat slices, using a serrated bread knife, then return the roll to the freezer at once.

Plain savoury crackers keep very well in an airtight container; cheese-flavoured biscuits will keep for about a week in this manner, or for up to 3 months in the freezer.

The storage life of cakes depends on type. Light sponges do not keep for long but light and rich fruit cakes will stay fresh in the tin for 2 weeks or more (some very rich types keep for several months). This chapter includes a popular mixed fruit loaf and classic cherry cake – both ideal for making individually or in batches. Keep them in an airtight container for a couple of weeks or freeze them for up to 3 months.

MAKING THE MOST OF HOME-BAKING

Here are just a few ideas for turning home-bakes from the pantry into clever impromptu dishes, snacks or light meals.

■ Savoury crackers and biscuits make excellent dippers – far better than crisps or salted bought savouries and ideal when there are no fresh vegetables in the refrigerator. For a really quick snack, serve them with mayonnaise, soft cheese or Greek yogurt mixed with finely grated hard cheese such as Cheddar or Parmesan. Add a little chopped spring onion or grated onion, with salt and pepper. Stir in a little grated eating apple, if available.

■ Top home-made crackers with a little mustard, add thin slices of cheese and grill briefly for an excellent cocktail snack. Anchovy paste or tomato purée may be used instead of mustard.

■ Use crumpets and muffins as mini pizza bases; top them with ham and cheese, then grill; top with poached or scrambled eggs; or top each with an open mushroom and halved bacon rasher, then grill.

■ Prick frozen doughnuts, place on dishes and soak with a little sherry, rum or orange liqueur. They thaw quickly at room temperature and make a delicious dessert when topped with cream or ice cream. Fresh or canned fruit may be added if available.

■ Crush home-made almond macaroons and stir into whipped cream with a little sherry. Divide between individual dishes and chill before serving. Top with a little grated chocolate or pieces of fruit.

JAM DOUGHNUTS

Home-made doughnuts are a real treat and they may be filled with the best-quality jam or a home-made preserve. Since the proving and deep frying is a time-consuming task, it is worth making a large batch and freezing them.

200 g/7 oz strong white flour
2.5 ml/½ tsp salt
150 g/5 oz caster sugar
10 ml/2 tsp dried yeast
2 eggs, beaten
50 g/2 oz butter, melted and slightly cooled
about 30 ml/2 tbsp firm jam for filling
oil for deep frying

Sift the flour and salt into a large mixing bowl. Stir in 50 g/2 oz of the sugar. Put about 30 ml/2 tbsp warm water in a bowl, sprinkle the dried yeast on top and leave for 10–15 minutes or until frothy.

Stir the eggs, butter and yeast liquid into the flour and mix to a soft dough. Turn on to a lightly floured surface and knead for about 5 minutes or until the dough is smooth and no longer sticky. Place in a large, lightly oiled polythene bag and leave in a warm place for about 1 hour or until the dough has doubled in bulk.

On a floured surface, roll the dough into a sausage shape and cut it into 12 equal portions. Flatten a portion of dough, place a little stiff jam in the centre, then pinch up the edges of the dough to form a ball and seal in the jam. Repeat with the remaining dough.

Place the dough balls on a floured baking sheet, flatten them slightly, then cover with a polythene bag and leave to rise for about 15 minutes or until light and puffy.

Heat the oil for deep frying to 185°C/360°F or until a bread cube immersed in the oil turns pale brown in 45 seconds. If using a deep-fat fryer, follow the manufacturer's instructions. Add the dough balls, a few at a time. Fry for about 5 minutes or until crisp and golden brown, turning frequently. Drain on absorbent kitchen paper. Toss in the remaining sugar.

MAKES 12

☆ **FREEZER TIP** Open freeze the doughnuts when cold, then pack them in a large bag when they are firm. They keep well for up to 6 months. Thaw individual doughnuts at room temperature or in the microwave for 30–60 seconds on High.

MUFFINS

The correct way to serve muffins is to split each one open around the edges almost to the centre. Toast slowly on both sides so that the heat penetrates to the centre, then pull the muffin halves apart, butter thickly, put together again and serve at once.

400 g/14 oz strong white flour
5 ml/1 tsp salt
25 g/1 oz butter or margarine
225 ml/7½ fl oz milk
10 ml/2 tsp dried yeast
1 egg
fat for frying

Sift the flour and salt into a large bowl. Rub in the butter or margarine. Place the milk in a saucepan and warm gently. It should be just hand-hot. Pour the milk into a small bowl, sprinkle the dried yeast on top and leave for 10–15 minutes until frothy. Beat in the egg.

Add the yeast liquid to the flour to make a very soft dough. Beat the dough by hand or with a wooden spoon for about 5 minutes until smooth and shiny. Cover the bowl with a large lightly oiled polythene bag and leave in a warm place for 1–2 hours or until doubled in bulk. Beat again lightly.

Roll out on a well floured surface to a thickness of about 1 cm/½ inch. Using a plain 7.5 cm/3 inch cutter, cut the dough into rounds. Place the rounds on a floured baking sheet, cover with polythene and leave to rise for about 45 minutes or until light and puffy.

Heat a griddle or heavy-bottomed frying pan, then grease it. Cook the muffins on both sides for about 8 minutes until golden.

MAKES 20

CRUMPETS

200 g/7 oz strong white flour
2.5 ml/½ tsp salt
2.5 ml/½ tsp sugar
100 ml/3½ fl oz milk
10 ml/2 tsp dried yeast
pinch of bicarbonate of soda
fat for frying

Sift the flour, salt and sugar into a large bowl. Place the milk in a saucepan, add 125 ml/4 fl oz water and warm gently. The mixture should be just hand-hot. Pour the mixture into a small bowl, sprinkle the dried yeast on top and leave for 10–15 minutes or until frothy.

Add the yeast liquid to the flour and beat to a smooth batter. Cover the bowl with a large lightly oiled polythene bag and leave in a warm place for about 45 minutes or until the batter has doubled in bulk.

Dissolve the bicarbonate of soda in 15 ml/1 tbsp warm water; beat into the batter. Cover and leave to rise again for 20 minutes.

Heat a griddle or heavy-bottomed frying pan over medium heat, then grease it when hot. Grease metal crumpet rings, poaching rings or large plain biscuit cutters about 7.5 cm/3 inches in diameter. Place the rings on the hot griddle, pour a spoonful of batter into each to cover the base thinly and cook until the top is set and the bubbles have burst.

Remove the rings and turn the crumpets over. Cook the other side for 2–3 minutes only, until firm but barely coloured. Cool the crumpets on a wire rack. Serve toasted, with butter.

MAKES 10 TO 12

CHERRY CAKE

Illustrated on page 35

fat for greasing
200 g/7 oz plain flour
1.25 ml/¼ tsp salt
2.5 ml/½ tsp baking powder
100 g/4 oz glacé cherries, quartered
150 g/5 oz butter or margarine
150 g/5 oz caster sugar
4 eggs
15 ml/1 tbsp milk (optional)

Line and grease a 15 cm/6 inch cake tin. Set the oven at 180°C/350°F/gas 4. Sift the flour, salt and baking powder into a bowl. Add the cherries and mix well. Set aside.

Place the butter or margarine in a mixing bowl and beat until very soft. Add the sugar and cream together until light and fluffy. Add the beaten eggs gradually, beating well after each addition. If the mixture shows signs of curdling, add a little of the flour mixture.

Fold in the dry ingredients lightly but thoroughly, adding the milk if too stiff.

Spoon into the prepared tin, level the surface and make a hollow in the centre, Bake for 30 minutes, then reduce the oven temperature to 160°C/325°F/gas 3 and bake for 50 minutes more until cooked through and firm to the touch. Cool on a wire rack.

MAKES ONE 15 CM/6 INCH CAKE

☕ **MRS BEETON'S TIP** When adding the cherries to the flour, be sure to mix them in thoroughly. If the cherries are coated in flour they will not sink to the bottom of the cake.

MIXED FRUIT LOAF

Illustrated on page 35

fat for greasing
200 g/7 oz self-raising flour
pinch of salt
100 g/4 oz margarine
100 g/4 oz caster sugar
grated rind of 1 orange
225 g/8 oz mixed dried fruit, eg 25 g/1 oz
    glacé cherries, 25 g/l oz cut mixed
    peel, 75 g/3 oz sultanas, 75 g/3 oz
    seedless raisins
1 egg
milk (see method)

Grease and line a 23 × 13 × 7.5 cm/ 9 × 5 × 3 inch loaf tin. Set the oven at 180°C/350°F/gas 4. Mix the flour and salt in a mixing bowl and rub in the margarine until the mixture resembles fine bread-crumbs. Stir in the sugar and orange rind. Cut the cherries, if used, into 4–6 pieces each, depending on size, and add with the remaining fruit.

In a measuring jug, beat the egg lightly and add enough milk to make up to 125 ml/ 4 fl oz. Add to the flour mixture, stir in, then mix well. Spoon into the prepared tin and bake for about 1 hour or until firm to the touch. Cool on a wire rack.

MAKES ONE 23 × 13 × 7.5 CM/ 9 × 5 × 3 INCH LOAF

☀ **MICROWAVE TIP** The dried fruit may be cleaned and plumped in a single operation in the microwave. Place the fruit in a bowl with cold water to cover. Heat on High until the water boils, allow to stand until cool enough to handle, then drain the fruit, removing any stalks.

ALMOND MACAROONS

fat for greasing
2 egg whites
150 g/5 oz caster sugar
100 g/4 oz ground almonds
10 ml/2 tsp ground rice
split almonds or halved glacé cherries to
    decorate

Grease a baking sheet and cover with rice paper. Set the oven at 160°C/325°F/ gas 3.

In a clean, grease-free bowl, whisk the egg whites until frothy but not stiff enough to form peaks. Stir in the sugar, ground almonds and ground rice. Beat with a wooden spoon until thick and white.

Place small spoonfuls of the mixture 5 cm/2 inches apart on the paper or pipe them on. Place a split almond or halved glacé cherry on each. Bake for 20 minutes or until pale fawn in colour. Cool on a wire rack.

MAKES 16 TO 20

RATAFIAS

fat for greasing
2 egg whites
150 g/5 oz caster sugar
100 g/4 oz ground almonds
10 ml/2 tsp ground rice

Grease a baking sheet and cover with rice paper. Set the oven at 160°C/325°F/ gas 3.

In a clean, grease-free bowl, whisk the egg whites until frothy but not stiff enough

to form peaks. Stir in the sugar, ground almonds and ground rice. Beat with a wooden spoon until thick and white.

Using a coffee spoon, place tiny heaps of the mixture on the rice paper, allowing a little room for spreading. The biscuits should be no more than 2 cm/¾ inch in diameter.

Bake for 10–12 minutes or until pale fawn in colour. Transfer to a wire rack and cool.

MAKES ABOUT 48

SPONGE FINGERS

fat for greasing
caster sugar for dusting
100 g/4 oz plain flour
pinch of salt
3 eggs, separated
100 g/4 oz caster sugar

Grease 18 sponge finger tins and dust lightly with caster sugar. Sift the flour with the salt. Set the oven at 160°C/325°F/gas 3.

Combine the egg yolks and sugar in a mixing bowl and beat together until pale and thick. Lightly fold in half the sifted flour mixture.

In a clean, grease-free bowl, whisk the egg whites to firm peaks. Fold very lightly into the yolk mixture with the remaining flour. Half fill the tins.

Bake for 12 minutes. Leave to cool slightly before transferring the sponge fingers to a wire rack to cool completely.

MAKES 18

BASIC WHITE BREAD

fat for greasing
800 g/1¾ lb strong white flour
10 ml/2 tsp salt
25 g/1 oz lard
25 g/1 oz fresh yeast or 15 ml/l tbsp dried
    yeast
2.5 ml/½ tsp sugar
flour for kneading
beaten egg or milk for glazing

Grease two 23 × 13 × 7.5 cm/9 × 5 × 3 inch loaf tins. Sift the flour and salt into a large bowl. Rub in the lard. Measure 500 ml/17 fl oz lukewarm water.

Blend the fresh yeast to a thin paste with the sugar and a little of the warm water. Set aside in a warm place until frothy – about 5 minutes. Sprinkle dried yeast over all the warm water and set aside until frothy, then stir well.

Add the yeast liquid and remaining water to the flour mixture and mix to a soft dough. Turn on to a floured surface and knead for about 8 minutes or until the dough is smooth, elastic and no longer sticky. Return to the bowl and cover with cling film. Leave in warm place until the dough has doubled in bulk – this will take up to 2 hours or longer.

Knead the dough again until firm. Cut into 2 equal portions and form each into a loaf shape. Place the dough in the prepared loaf tins and brush the surface with beaten egg or milk. Place the tins in a large, lightly oiled polythene bag. Leave in a warm place for about 45 minutes or until the dough has doubled in bulk. Set the oven at 230°C/450°F/gas 8.

Bake for 35–40 minutes, until the loaves are crisp and golden brown, and sound hollow when tapped on the bottom.

MAKES TWO 800 G/1¾ LB LOAVES

CRISP CRACKERS

Illustrated on page 36

fat for greasing
225 g/8 oz plain flour
2.5 ml/½ tsp salt
about 125 ml/4 fl oz milk
1 egg yolk, beaten

Grease 2 baking sheets. Set the oven at 180°C/350°F/gas 4. Sift the flour and salt into a bowl, then make a well in the middle and add about half the milk. Add the egg yolk to the milk and gradually work in the flour to make a firm dough, adding more milk as necessary.

Turn the dough out on to a lightly floured surface and knead it briefly until it is perfectly smooth. Divide the piece of dough in half and wrap one piece in cling film to prevent it from drying out while you roll out the other piece.

Roll out the dough very thinly and use a 7.5 cm/3 inch round cutter to stamp out crackers. Gather up the trimmings and re-roll them. Place the crackers on the prepared baking sheets. Bake for 12–18 minutes, until golden. Transfer the crackers to a wire rack to cool.

MAKES ABOUT 24

CHEESE STRAWS

fat for greasing
100 g/4 oz plain flour
pinch of mustard powder
pinch of salt
pinch of cayenne pepper
75 g/3 oz butter
75 g/3 oz grated Parmesan cheese
1 egg yolk
flour for rolling out

Grease 4 baking sheets. Set the oven at 200°C/400°F/gas 6.

Sift the flour, mustard, salt and cayenne into a bowl. In a mixing bowl, cream the butter until soft and white, then add the flour mixture with the cheese. Stir in the egg yolk and enough cold water to form a stiff dough.

Roll out on a lightly floured surface to a thickness of about 5 mm/¼ inch and cut into fingers, each measuring about 10 × 1 cm/4 × ½ inch. From the pastry trimmings make several rings, each about 4 cm/1½ inches in diameter.

With a palette knife, transfer both rings and straws to the prepared baking sheets and bake for 8–10 minutes or until lightly browned and crisp. Cool on the baking sheets.

To serve, fit a few straws through each ring and lay the bundles in the centre of a plate with any remaining straws crisscrossed around them.

MAKES 48 TO 60

CARAWAY CRACKERS

Illustrated on page 36

Originally, these simple biscuits were sweetened with 50 g/2 oz caster sugar but the flavour of the caraway seeds makes such an excellent savoury cracker that the sugar is omitted in this recipe. However, if you particularly like the flavour of caraway you may like to try the old recipe and add the sugar to the flour. If you are making the savoury crackers try using brown flour instead of white.

fat for greasing
50 g/2 oz butter
225 g/8 oz plain flour
15 g/½ oz caraway seeds
good pinch of salt
1 egg, beaten
milk to glaze

Grease 2 baking sheets. Set the oven at 180°C/350°F/gas 4. Place the butter in a small bowl and beat it until it is very soft. Gradually beat in the flour, caraway seeds and salt until the ingredients are thoroughly mixed.

Add the beaten egg and mix well to make a firm dough. Knead the dough briefly on a floured surface, then roll it out thinly and cut out 5 cm/2 inch circles.

Place the crackers on the baking sheets and brush them with a little milk, then bake them for about 12–15 minutes. Transfer the crackers to a wire rack to cool.

MAKES ABOUT 30

GRISSINI

These crunchy Italian bread sticks are delicious served at the beginning of a meal with the soup or starter.

fat for greasing
400 g/14 oz strong white flour
5 ml/1 tsp salt
25 g/1 oz margarine
50 ml/2 fl oz milk
15 g/½ oz fresh yeast or 10 ml/2 tsp dried yeast
2.5 ml/½ tsp sugar
flour for kneading
beaten egg white or milk for glazing
sesame seeds, poppy seeds or salt (optional)

Grease a baking sheet. Sift the flour and salt into a large bowl. Rub in the margarine. Warm the milk and 200 ml/7 fl oz water until lukewarm.

Blend the fresh yeast to a thin paste with the sugar and a little of the warm liquid. Set aside in a warm place until frothy – about 5 minutes. Sprinkle the dried yeast over all the liquid until frothy, then stir well.

Add the yeast liquid and remaining liquid to the flour and mix to a soft dough. Turn on to a lightly floured surface and knead for about 5 minutes or until the dough is smooth and no longer sticky. Return to the bowl and cover with cling film. Leave in a warm place until the dough has doubled in bulk – this will take up to 2 hours, or longer.

Set the oven at 220°C/425°F/gas 7. Knead the dough again until firm. Cut into 15 g/½ oz pieces. Roll each piece into a strand 32 cm/13 inches long. Place the strands on the prepared baking sheet. Brush the surface of each with beaten egg white or milk, then sprinkle, if liked, with the seeds or salt. Place the baking sheet in a large lightly oiled polythene bag. Leave in a warm place for 10 minutes. Bake for 10–15 minutes, until golden brown and very crisp.

MAKES ABOUT 45 STICKS

OATCAKES

Illustrated on page 36

fat for greasing
50 g/2 oz bacon fat or dripping
100 g/4 oz medium oatmeal
1.25 ml/¼ tsp salt
1.25 ml/¼ tsp bicarbonate of soda
fine oatmeal for rolling out

Grease 2 baking sheets. Set the oven at 160°C/325°F/gas 3.

Melt the bacon fat or dripping in a large saucepan. Remove from the heat and stir in the dry ingredients, then add enough boiling water to make a stiff dough.

When cool enough to handle, knead the dough thoroughly, then roll out on a surface dusted with fine oatmeal, to a thickness of 5 mm/¼ inch. Cut into wedge-shaped pieces and transfer to the prepared baking sheets. Bake for 20–30 minutes. Cool on a wire rack.

MAKES ABOUT 16

COOKING WITH DRIED AND CANNED FOODS

These are the traditional storecupboard items. Alongside chutneys, pickles and salted vegetables they were once essential winter foods: today they are the basis for a wide variety of interesting dishes. This chapter also offers ideas for using easy-to-store canned foods to best advantage.

Foods preserved by ancient methods are now important ingredients in their own right – prunes, figs, raisins and other dried fruits have more potential than as ingredients for baking. Dried pulses, vegetables and cereals are all essential storecupboard ingredients for everyday cooking.

DRIED FOODS

The majority of dried foods keep well for months, if not years; it is however always wise to check details on the packet as some cereals and grains can become rancid in comparatively short periods.

Planning a Store There are two main types of dried foods: those that are ready to use and those that require lengthy pre-soaking. The majority of fruits and vegetables are now available in a ready-to-use form. Pulses such as lentils do not require soaking, while others, including haricots, flageolets and black-eye beans, will cook successfully, if not quickly, without soaking. Cereals such as cracked wheat are soon prepared, whereas whole wheat grain requires longer cooking.

In planning a useful store, try to include some foods that can be cooked quickly as well as others that need soaking or long boiling.

Dried mushrooms, onions and peppers are useful standbys. Dried mushrooms, particularly Italian, Chinese or wild varieties, contribute a distinctive flavour and can be used to transform plain ingredients into special meals.

Unless you bake frequently, you may not want to keep a wide selection of dried fruit. If this is the case raisins and apricots are the most versatile choice as they combine well with savoury or sweet foods. If you do not have a freezer, dried apple rings or fruit salad are also useful.

Always keep dried foods in airtight containers in a cool, dark place and remember to rotate supplies, bringing older stocks to the front of the cupboard from time to time. Never top up half empty jars with new supplies.

CANNED FOODS

Canning and other methods of heat preservation provide an ever-increasing selection of products, far too broad to list or discuss in detail. When planning a useful stock of canned goods, consider which you use most often; standard ingredients like tomatoes, rather than emergency supplies, as well as others that save time when you are in a hurry or may be substituted for out-of-stock fresh foods.

Everyday Ingredients Canned beans and pulses are particularly useful. Kidney beans and chick peas are excellent quality and not mushy. The range extends far beyond these two items; most varieties are good, although canned haricot and butter beans can be disappointing.

Tomatoes, particularly chopped tomatoes, sweetcorn, canned fish and canned meats such as corned beef are also useful storecupboard ingredients.

Emergency Stores These are the items to rely upon when you forget vital items when shopping or need to make supper in a hurry. Mushrooms (creamed varieties are sometimes superior to those canned in water), basic sauces, cream (useful in desserts and sparingly in savoury cooking), soups, including consommé, cooked rice, custard (for fools, ice creams, trifles and so on), rice pudding (for desserts) are all worth stocking. Heat treated milk (UHT) is a useful basic item.

USING CANNED AND DRIED FOOD

■ Once opened canned food should be treated as fresh and used promptly. Leftovers should be transferred to a covered dish and chilled.

■ Similarly, reconstituted dried foods should be treated as fresh and used at once or chilled.

■ The liquid in which some dried foods were soaked may often be used for flavouring dishes. This applies as much to mushrooms and onions as it does to fruit soaking liquid.

■ Always boil dried beans rapidly for 10 minutes to destroy natural toxins which could otherwise cause food poisoning, then reduce the heat and continue cooking until tender.

■ It is important to check cooking instructions for unfamiliar dried items or when heating prepared products. Many sauces or soups, for instance, should not be boiled. Overcooking canned foods is a common fault; remember that they are already cooked and simply need heating.

HOME DRYING

For certain success, it is essential to dry foods using a dehydrator; however, items such as mushrooms or apple rings may be long-dried in a cool oven, provided they are constantly monitored.

A dehydrator, consisting of a heating element, fan and layers of racks makes the drying process safe and easy. Mushrooms, fruit, fruit purées and vegetables may all be dried successfully by this method.

It is important that the manufacturer's instructions are followed and that the dried food is stored in airtight containers in a cool, dark place after processing.

MUESLI

200 g/7 oz mixed grains, such as natural
    wheat bran, maize meal, wheat meal
    and oat flakes
30 ml/2 tbsp chopped mixed nuts
30 ml/2 tbsp raisins
30 ml/2 tbsp dried apple flakes
12 dried apricots
30 ml/2 tbsp soft light brown sugar

Mix all the ingredients together and store in a sealed polythene tub or airtight jar until required.

SERVES 4 TO 6

CURRIED BEANS

200 g/7 oz dried haricot beans, soaked
    overnight in water to cover
30 ml/2 tbsp oil
1 onion, finely chopped
2.5 cm/1 inch piece of fresh root ginger,
    peeled and finely chopped
2 garlic cloves, crushed
pinch of cayenne pepper
15 ml/1 tbsp ground coriander
2.5 ml/½ tsp turmeric
30 ml/2 tbsp brown sugar
1 (397 g/14 oz) can chopped tomatoes
1 bay leaf
salt and pepper
50 g/2 oz raisins
1 eating apple, peeled, cored and diced

Drain the beans, put them in a clean saucepan and add fresh water to cover. Bring the water to the boil, boil briskly for 10 minutes, then lower the heat and simmer the beans for about 40 minutes or until just tender.

Meanwhile heat the oil in a large saucepan. Fry the onion, ginger and garlic over gentle heat for about 10 minutes. Stir in cayenne to taste, with the coriander, turmeric and sugar. Fry for 5 minutes more, stirring constantly.

Drain the beans and add them, with the canned tomatoes and bay leaf, to the onion mixture. Add salt and pepper to taste and stir well. Bring just to the boil, then reduce the heat and simmer for 30 minutes. Add the raisins and apple, re-cover and cook gently for a further 30 minutes.

SERVES 4

SPICED LENTILS

450 g/1 lb red lentils
2.5 ml/½ tsp sea salt
45 ml/3 tbsp oil
1 onion, chopped
1 small cooking apple, chopped
1.25 ml/¼ tsp turmeric
1.25 ml/¼ tsp ground ginger
10 ml/2 tsp garam masala
5 ml/1 tsp ground cumin
3 tomatoes, peeled and chopped

GARNISH
    chopped fresh coriander leaves
    fried onion rings (optional)

Put the lentils in a large saucepan with 900 ml/1½ pints water. Bring to the boil, lower the heat and cover the pan. Simmer gently for 20 minutes. Add the sea salt and simmer for 5 minutes more or until the lentils are soft and all the water has been absorbed.

Meanwhile, heat the oil in a large deep frying pan and add the onion, apple and spices. Fry gently for about 10 minutes until the vegetables are soft and lightly browned. Stir in the tomatoes and cook for 5 minutes, then pour in the lentils.

Stir thoroughly, then serve very hot, sprinkled with the coriander leaves and onion rings, if liked.

SERVES 4 TO 6

> **MRS BEETON'S TIP** To peel tomatoes, cut a small cross in the top of each fruit and place them in a bowl. Pour on freshly boiling water. Leave for about 45 seconds, depending on ripeness, then drain. Peel back and remove the skins.

FELAFEL

Illustrated on page 69

Serve felafel in pitta pockets, or omit the tahini and serve with Greek yogurt and salad for a simple and satisfying lunch.

200 g/7 oz chick peas, soaked overnight or
 for several hours in water to cover
75 g/3 oz fine matzo meal or wholemeal
 flour
5 ml/1 tsp salt
5 ml/1 tsp ground cumin
10 ml/2 tsp ground coriander
1 garlic clove, crushed
oil for deep frying

TAHINI SAUCE
50 g/2 oz ground sesame seeds
1 garlic clove, crushed
1.25 ml/¼ tsp salt
15 ml/1 tbsp lemon juice
pinch of pepper

Drain the chick peas, put them in a clean saucepan and add fresh water to cover. Bring to the boil, lower the heat and simmer for 1–2 hours until very tender. Drain, mince the chick peas finely or chop and sieve them.

Combine the minced chick peas, matzo meal, salt, cumin, coriander and garlic in a bowl. Form into small balls, adding 15–30 ml/1–2 tbsp water if necessary.

Heat the oil to 170°C/338°F or until a cube of bread added to the oil browns in 1½ minutes. Add the felafel, a few at a time, and fry until golden brown. Drain on absorbent kitchen paper; keep hot while cooking successive batches.

To make the tahini sauce, mix all the ingredients together and add 75 ml/5 tbsp water. Sieve to a smooth purée or process in a blender or food processor for a few minutes. Add more salt and pepper if required.

MAKES 36

HUMMUS

Illustrated on page 69

Serve as a starter or snack, with French bread, pitta or crispbreads.

150 g/5 oz chick peas
1 garlic clove, chopped
salt
90 ml/6 tbsp olive oil
60 ml/4 tbsp Tahini (bought or see recipe
 left)
60 ml/4 tbsp lemon juice
chopped parsley to garnish

Soak and cook the chick peas, following the method given for Felafel, left. Drain thoroughly, then mash and sieve or crush in a mortar with a pestle to a smooth paste. An alternative, and much easier method is to process the chick peas in a blender or food processor.

Add the garlic and salt to taste. Stir briskly until well mixed, then gradually work in the olive oil, as when making mayonnaise. The chick peas should form a creamy paste. Slowly work in the tahini, adding it a teaspoonful at a time at first. When the mixture is creamy work in lemon juice to taste.

Transfer the hummus to a shallow serving bowl and sprinkle with chopped parsley.

SERVES 6 TO 8

SPAGHETTI ALLA CARBONARA

Illustrated on page 70

450 g/1 lb spaghetti
salt and pepper
15 ml/1 tbsp oil
100 g/4 oz rindless streaky bacon rashers,
   cut in fine strips
4 eggs
30 ml/2 tbsp double cream
75 g/3 oz Pecorino or Parmesan cheese,
   grated

Cook the spaghetti in a large saucepan of boiling salted water for 8–10 minutes or until tender but still firm to the bite.

Meanwhile heat the oil in a large frying pan and fry the bacon until the fat is transparent. Draw the pan off the heat. In a bowl, beat the eggs with the cream, adding a little salt and a generous grinding of pepper.

Drain the cooked spaghetti thoroughly and mix it with the bacon. Return to moderate heat for 1–2 minutes to heat through. Stir the egg mixture rapidly into the pan. As it begins to thicken, tip in the cheese. Do not stir it in. Serve immediately on hot plates.

SERVES 4

MRS BEETON'S TIP Use fresh pasta with this sauce, if preferred. It will cook in considerably less time than dried pasta and will be ready as soon as it rises to the surface of the boiling water. Test after 1 minute.

MACARONI CHEESE

An old favourite, Macaroni Cheese may be served solo or with grilled bacon or sausages. A layer of sliced tomato may be added to the topping before being baked or grilled, if liked.

fat for greasing
150 g/5 oz elbow-cut macaroni
salt and pepper
25 g/1 oz butter
100 g/4 oz Cheddar cheese, grated

WHITE SAUCE
50 g/2 oz butter
50 g/2 oz plain flour
600 ml/1 pint milk

Grease a 750 ml/1¼ pint pie dish. Set the oven at 200°C/400°F/gas 6. Cook the macaroni in a large saucepan of boiling salted water for 10–12 minutes or until tender but still firm to the bite.

Meanwhile make the white sauce. Melt the butter in a large saucepan, stir in the flour and cook over low heat for 2–3 minutes. Do not allow the mixture to colour. Gradually add the milk, stirring constantly until the mixture boils and thickens.

Drain the macaroni thoroughly and stir it gently into the white sauce. Add three quarters of the cheese, with salt and pepper to taste. Spoon the mixture into the prepared pie dish. Sprinkle with the remaining cheese and bake for 15–20 minutes.

Alternatively, place under a preheated grill for 2–4 minutes to melt and brown the cheese topping.

SERVES 3 TO 4

FLAGEOLET BEAN SALAD

The fresh green colour and tender flavour of flageolets makes them an ideal candidate for a light summer salad. Add a little crumbled grilled bacon or drained flaked tuna and serve with French bread for a simple summer lunch.

225 g/8 oz dried flageolet beans, soaked
    overnight in water to cover
1 bouquet garni
150 ml/¼ pint mayonnaise
1 onion, finely chopped
15 ml/1 tbsp finely chopped parsley
salt

Drain the beans, put them in a clean saucepan with the bouquet garni and add fresh water to cover. Bring the water to the boil, boil briskly for 10 minutes, then lower the heat and simmer the beans for 1¼–1½ hours until tender.

Drain the beans thoroughly, remove the bouquet garni and tip into a bowl. While the beans are still warm, stir in the mayonnaise, onion and parsley, with salt to taste. Toss lightly.

Allow the salad to stand for at least 3 hours before serving to allow the flavours to blend.

SERVES 4 TO 6

MRS BEETON'S TIP Do not add salt to the water when cooking pulses such as dried flageolet beans as it toughens them. Pulses are delicious when cooked in vegetable stock, but take care to use a salt-free variety.

LENTIL AND ONION SALAD

225 g/8 oz brown or green lentils, soaked
    for 2–3 hours in water to cover
1 salt-free vegetable or onion stock cube
sea salt
1 red onion, thinly sliced in rings
2 tablespoons finely chopped parsley

DRESSING
    45 ml/3 tbsp light olive oil
    salt and pepper
    pinch of mustard powder
    pinch of caster sugar
    5 ml/1 tsp soy sauce
    15 ml/1 tbsp red wine vinegar

Put the lentils in a saucepan with cold water to cover. Bring to the boil, add the crumbled stock cube, lower the heat and simmer for 30–40 minutes until tender but not mushy.

Meanwhile make the dressing by shaking all the ingredients together in a tightly closed screw-topped jar.

Drain the cooked lentils thoroughly, tip into a serving bowl and immediately add the dressing. Toss lightly, then add the onion rings with half the parsley.

Allow the salad to stand for at least 1 hour before serving to allow the flavours to blend. Sprinkle with the remaining parsley.

SERVES 4 TO 6

MRS BEETON'S TIP Italian red onions are at their best in late spring. Mild, sweet and crisp, they are ideal for stuffing, roasting whole or serving in salads.

RICE AND ARTICHOKE SALAD

Basmati rice gives this salad the best flavour. Make the vinaigrette at least 1 hour before use, to allow the flavours to develop.

200 g/7 oz long-grain rice
salt
100 ml/3½ fl oz Vinaigrette Dressing
    (page 56)
1 garlic clove, crushed
1 (397 g/14 oz) can artichoke hearts,
    drained
    and halved
30 ml/2 tbsp snipped chives to garnish

Place the rice in a saucepan and pour in 450 ml/¾ pint cold water. Add a little salt, then bring to the boil. Cover the pan tightly and reduce the heat to the lowest setting. Leave the rice for 15 minutes, turn off the heat and leave for a further 15 minutes without removing the lid.

Mix the dressing and garlic, add to the hot rice and fork it in lightly. Leave to cool.

Just before serving, fork the artichoke hearts into the rice. Sprinkle with the chives.

SERVES 4

———————— ◈ ————————

PASTA, ANCHOVY AND SWEETCORN SALAD

Illustrated on page 70

150 g/5 oz pasta shells
salt and pepper
60 ml/4 tbsp mayonnaise
1 (50 g/2 oz) can anchovies, drained and
    finely chopped
225 g/8 oz drained canned sweetcorn
    kernels
2 spring onions, finely chopped, to
    garnish

Cook the pasta in a large saucepan of boiling salted water for 10–12 minutes or until tender but still firm to the bite. Drain thoroughly. While still warm, stir in the mayonnaise. Set aside to cool.

Add the anchovies and sweetcorn, with salt and pepper to taste. Toss the salad lightly and garnish with the chopped spring onions.

SERVES 4 TO 6

> **MRS BEETON'S TIP** Use any decorative pasta for this dish. Spirals, bows or tiny cartwheels are all suitable. For a touch of colour, use tomato or spinach-flavoured pasta shapes.

SAVOURY RICE

200 g/7 oz long-grain rice
1 onion, chopped
salt and pepper
50 g/2 oz mature Cheddar cheese, grated
45 ml/3 tbsp Fresh Tomato Sauce (page 57)
30 ml/2 tbsp chopped parsley
1.25 ml/¼ tsp dried mixed herbs
pinch of cayenne pepper
50 g/2 oz butter, chopped
25 g/1 oz Parmesan cheese, grated, to serve

Place the rice and onion in a saucepan and pour in 450 ml/¾ pint cold water. Add a little salt. Bring to the boil, cover the pan tightly and reduce the heat to the lowest setting. Leave for 15 minutes, turn off the heat and leave for a further 15 minutes without removing the lid.

Mix in the cheese and tomato sauce, with the parsley, herbs, cayenne and salt and pepper to taste. Stir in the butter. Heat through, stirring, for 3–4 minutes, then pile on to a warmed serving dish. Sprinkle with Parmesan cheese and serve at once.

SERVES 3 TO 4

> **MRS BEETON'S TIP** Buy Parmesan cheese in the block, if possible. If you buy from a reputable supplier, the cheese will not be unacceptably hard. Store it in the refrigerator, sealed in a polythene bag, and grate it yourself when required. The flavour will be superior to that of the pre-packaged grated cheese. Alternatively, grate freshly bought cheese and freeze it – it may be used from frozen.

BUCKWHEAT AND CHEESE PUDDING

Buckwheat, the seed of a plant which is thought to have originated in China, is nutritious and high in fibre. The seeds are sold hulled and roasted, but must be cooked before being used in a recipe.

fat for greasing
200 g/7 oz roasted buckwheat
1 egg
75 g/3 oz butter
salt and pepper
75 g/3 oz Parmesan cheese, grated

Grease a 900 ml/1½ pint baking dish. Set the oven at 190°C/375°F/gas 5. Put the buckwheat into a large saucepan with 600 ml/1 pint cold water. Bring to the boil, turn the heat to the lowest setting and cover the pan tightly. Leave for 15 minutes by which time the grains should have absorbed all the liquid.

Tip the buckwheat into a bowl, add the egg and beat well. Stir in 25 g/1 oz of the butter and seasoning. Melt the remaining butter in a small pan.

Put alternate layers of buckwheat and grated cheese in the prepared baking dish. Pour the remaining butter over the top. Bake for 20–30 minutes, until browned.

SERVES 3 TO 4

———————— ◇ ————————

SALAD DRESSINGS, SAUCES AND STUFFINGS

**Clever use of dressings, sauces and stuffings can transform
plain ingredients into special meals, so it is worth having
chilled or frozen preparations in stock at all times. Even
items that are partially prepared, such as flavoured vinegars
and oils or stuffing bases, save time and serve as an
inspiration when time is at a premium.**

When it comes to storing dressings, stuffings and sauces for future use, it makes sense to prepare a large batch of a versatile recipe which lends itself to many uses, rather than to make a complicated concoction with limited usefulness. This way you will always have something to pep up plain fish fillets, cheer up chops or toss into a simple salad.

CHILLING OR FREEZING

Oils and vinegars have a long shelf life, so they do not need chilling or freezing. When combined with other ingredients, such as herbs, spices, onion and garlic, they act as preservatives, allowing dressings to be stored chilled or at least kept cool for long periods.

Stuffing mixes made from thoroughly dried breadcrumbs and other dry ingredients, may be kept successfully chilled in an airtight container for long periods; however, the better method is to prepare a fresh stuffing and freeze it. A batch of fresh breadcrumb mix may be frozen and the required amount spooned out of the pack to use as required. Fresh ingredients and liquid may then be added but the time-consuming task of crumbing bread and chopping herbs will already have been done.

Many fresh sauces keep for 3–5 days if cooled and chilled promptly after cooking. This can be useful if you intend making several dishes over a long weekend, for example, when a basic tomato sauce can be adapted to pizza topping, seafood casserole or a meaty goulash. In the long term, frozen tomato sauce may be thawed in the microwave or in a covered pan over the lowest possible heat. Once thawed, the sauce can be heated and used as a side dish or as the basis for more a complicated recipe.

This chapter includes one sauce that should reside in every herb-lover's refrigerator: pesto. Grow a huge tub of basil outdoors in the summer to use as required and at the end of the summer you should still have enough to make a few pots of pesto. Olive oil is the essential preservative, so do not skimp on quantity. Make sure jars are perfectly clean and check the sauce after a couple of days to ensure it has a good layer of oil on the surface. In this state it will keep at the bottom of the refrigerator for several months, although once opened and partially used it should be eaten quickly.

Another sauce of Italian origin, tonnato or tuna sauce, is the ideal emergency recipe. It consists of tuna creamed to a mayonnaise-like consistency and can be used to coat cooked veal, chicken, pasta, eggs or vegetables.

Caramel and chocolate are two sweet sauces that have long refrigerator lives; they are always useful as toppings for ice cream, sponge cake, meringues or fresh fruit.

FLAVOURED OILS AND VINEGARS

When making dressings for long storage, remember that the flavour of garlic, spices or other strong ingredients will become very pronounced on standing, so they are often best added just before use. However, oils and vinegars flavoured with herbs and spices are a good standby. Recipes for horseradish and fruit vinegars are given on pages 138 and 139; here are some alternative suggestions:

Herbs Use sprigs of fresh herbs to flavour oil or vinegar. Trim off excess stalk or use the leaves only if they are large (such as bay or sage). Wash thoroughly and dry on absorbent kitchen paper. Place several herb sprigs or leaves in a clean dry bottle, bending and crushing bay or sage to bring out the flavour. Cover with a light oil, such as grapeseed or sunflower, or use vinegar. Wine or cider vinegar is ideal for tarragon and other herbs. A strong vinegar, such as balsamic, may be used with bay, thyme, marjoram, rosemary and other herbs which have a pronounced flavour.

Cover the bottles tightly and leave in a cool, dark place for at least 2 weeks to allow the flavour to infuse.

Spices Chilli and garlic are popular flavourings for oil and vinegar. Dried red chillies should be added sparingly to bottles of oil or vinegar and allowed to infuse for a couple of weeks. One or two chillies to 600 ml/1 pint gives plenty of flavour but this can be increased for very hot results. This is a particularly useful way of flavouring oil for stir frying or for use in spicy dishes. Opt for a versatile oil, such as sunflower, which may be used in cooking as well as dressings.

Whole peeled garlic cloves may be added to vinegar for flavouring salad dressings at a later stage. Garlic-flavoured oil is useful for cooking.

A spiced vinegar recipe for pickling is given on page 138 but individual spices may be added to bottles of oil or vinegar, if liked. Try adding a cinnamon stick, a few cloves, crushed coriander seeds or crushed allspice berries.

USING FLAVOURED OILS AND VINEGARS

■ Toss a little flavoured oil or vinegar into a salad before dressing with soured cream or mayonnaise.

■ Use to make salad dressings, either on their own or with unflavoured oil. A little flavoured oil may be used to make mayonnaise but should be blended with plain oil or the result may be too strongly flavoured.

■ Trickle garlic or chilli oil over slices of French bread, bake until golden, then serve as a snack or as an accompaniment with soup.

■ Flavour cider vinegar strongly with herbs; use sparingly in sauces, adding it to taste just before serving. For example, make a sweetened apple sauce to serve with pork, then give it a herby sweet-sour tang by adding rosemary or sage vinegar.

■ Mint vinegar may be used to flavour sweetened fruit drinks or dessert sauces.

STORING AND USING STUFFINGS

The simplest stuffing combination to store or freeze consists of breadcrumbs with parsley and thyme. Unless both herbs and crumbs are thoroughly dried, they should be frozen. When freezing any stuffing always include a detailed label. Although you may be convinced that you will remember exactly how the aromatic lemon and raisin stuffing was made, three months later you will probably have difficulty in deciding whether it is appropriate for fish steaks or more suitable for poultry.

The types of stuffings which freeze well in large quantities are the ones that go well with everything. Consider these combinations:

■ Breadcrumbs or cooked rice with lemon rind, chopped parsley, raisins and parsley. Good with cod steaks, chicken, duck, pork chops or lamb.

■ Wholemeal breadcrumbs with marjoram, peeled and chopped tomato, and par-cooked finely chopped onion. Open freeze the mixture to prevent it from forming a lump, then break it up and pack. Use with pork, lamb or in beef olives (rolled slices of meat). The stuffing may also be mixed with minced beef, lamb or pork to make meat loaf, burgers or meatballs.

■ Lightly cooked finely chopped onion and garlic mixed with grated fresh root ginger and a little chopped green chilli makes a good flavouring. Mix with breadcrumbs, a sprinkling of ground coriander and a little chopped fresh coriander to create an excellent spicy stuffing for chicken breasts or lamb breast. Mixed with minced lamb, it makes delicious meatballs.

■ Breadcrumbs or cooked lentils, grated orange rind, thyme or rosemary, parsley and cooked finely chopped onion is another winning mixture. Open freeze, then pack in chunks. Use with pork, lamb, duck or vegetables. Add some finely chopped nuts and use to make vegetarian burgers.

■ Mixed with grated cheese, breadcrumb stuffing mixes make excellent gratin toppings or toppings for savoury crumble.

■ Use breadcrumb mixes to coat chicken breasts, then bake until cooked and golden.

VINAIGRETTE DRESSING

90 ml/6 tbsp light olive oil
salt and pepper
pinch of mustard powder
pinch of caster sugar
30 ml/2 tbsp white wine vinegar
10 ml/2 tsp finely chopped gherkin
5 ml/1 tsp finely chopped onion or chives
5 ml/1 tsp finely chopped parsley
5 ml/1 tsp finely chopped capers
5 ml/1 tsp finely chopped tarragon or
   chervil

Mix all the ingredients together in a screw-topped jar. Close tightly, shake well, then allow to stand for at least 1 hour to allow the flavours to blend. Shake again before using.

MAKES ABOUT 125 ML/4 FL OZ

FRENCH DRESSING

Illustrated on page 71

90 ml/6 tbsp olive oil or a mixture of olive
    oil and sunflower oil
salt and pepper
pinch of mustard powder
pinch of caster sugar
30 ml/2 tbsp wine vinegar

Mix all the ingredients together in a
screw-topped jar. Close tightly. Shake well
before using.

MAKES ABOUT 125 ML/4 FL OZ

VARIATIONS

Almost every cook has his or her favourite
way of preparing French dressing. Garlic,
whole or crushed, is a favourite addition,
while others swear that a few drops of
soy sauce sharpen the flavour. Lemon
juice frequently replaces all or part of the
vinegar. The recipe above may be doubled
or trebled, if liked, but the proportions
should always remain the same.

CHIFFONADE DRESSING

Illustrated on page 71

2 hard-boiled eggs, finely chopped
½ small red pepper, seeded and finely
    chopped
30 ml/2 tbsp finely chopped parsley
5 ml/1 tsp very finely chopped shallot
125 ml/4 fl oz French dressing (recipe
    above)

Mix all the ingredients in a small bowl.
Whisk with a balloon whisk to blend
thoroughly.

MAKES 150 ML/¼ PINT

CLARET DRESSING

Illustrated on page 71

1 garlic clove, crushed
125 ml/4 fl oz claret
5 ml/1 tsp lemon juice
5 ml/1 tsp finely chopped shallot or onion
salt and pepper

Mix all the ingredients together in a
screw-topped jar. Close tightly. Shake well,
then allow to stand overnight to allow the
flavours to blend. Shake, strain and pour
over a salad tossed in a little oil.

MAKES ABOUT 150 ML/¼ PINT

FRESH TOMATO SAUCE

30 ml/2 tbsp olive oil
1 onion, finely chopped
1 garlic clove, crushed
1 rindless streaky bacon rasher, chopped
800 g/1¾ lb tomatoes, peeled and
    chopped
salt and pepper
pinch of sugar
15 ml/1 tbsp chopped fresh basil or 5 ml/
    1 tsp dried basil

Heat the oil in a saucepan and fry the
onion, garlic and bacon over gentle heat for
5 minutes. Stir in the remaining
ingredients except the basil, cover the
pan and simmer gently for 30 minutes.

Rub the sauce through a sieve into a clean
saucepan or purée in a blender or food
processor until smooth. Add the basil.
Reheat the sauce. Check the seasoning
before serving and add more salt and
pepper if required.

MAKES ABOUT 600 ML/1 PINT

PESTO GENOVESE

Illustrated on page 72

A little pesto goes a long way to flavour pasta. Put the pasta in a heated serving bowl or individual dishes, add the pesto and toss lightly. Serve at once.

2 garlic cloves, roughly chopped
25–40 g/1–1½ oz fresh basil leaves, roughly chopped
25 g/1 oz pine nuts, chopped
40 g/1½ oz Parmesan cheese, grated
juice of 1 lemon
salt and pepper
75–100 ml/3–3½ fl oz olive oil

Combine the garlic, basil leaves, nuts, cheese, lemon juice, salt and pepper in a mortar. Pound with a pestle until smooth. Alternatively, process in a blender or food processor. While blending, trickle in the oil as when making mayonnaise, until the sauce forms a very thick paste.

SERVES 4

MRS BEETON'S TIP Basil has a particular affinity with Italian dishes and it is worth growing it in a large pot on the patio during summer. For a simple starter with a wonderful taste, try sliced tomatoes topped with mozzarella cheese, a drizzle of olive oil and chopped fresh basil leaves.

TUNA SAUCE

Illustrated on page 72

The pantry furnishes all the ingredients for this excellent sauce. It is traditionally used to coat cold cooked veal, but is equally good with hard-boiled eggs, cold cooked chicken, pasta or over brown rice.

1 (198 g/7 oz) can tuna in oil
juice of 1 lemon
2 anchovy fillets, roughly chopped
100 ml/3½ fl oz olive oil
Salt and pepper
15 ml/1 tbsp capers, chopped

Place the tuna, with the oil from the can, in a mixing bowl. Add the lemon juice and anchovy fillets and mash finely with a wooden spoon until smooth. Alternatively, process in a blender or food processor.

When the mixture is smooth, trickle in the oil gradually, as when making mayonnaise, whisking vigorously or blending at high speed until the mixture thickens. Add salt and pepper to taste. Fold in the capers.

MAKES ABOUT 200 ML/7 FL OZ

MRS BEETON'S TIP There is a wide range of olive oils on the market, from the rich green extra-virgin oil to light, mild but equally flavoursome oils specially formulated for frying, cooking and baking. It is always worth buying a good quality oil and experimenting to find the flavour that suits your family best. Store olive oil in a cool dark place, if necessary decanting it into a clean green glass wine bottle with cork to protect it from ultravoilet rays.

HERB STUFFING

Keeping a stock of stuffing in the freezer means that chicken, fish fillets and boned joints can swiftly be prepared for the oven. Use double the quantity listed below when stuffing the neck end of a 5–6 kg/11–13 lb turkey.

50 g/2 oz butter or margarine
100 g/4 oz soft white or Granary
    breadcrumbs
pinch of grated nutmeg
15 ml/1 tbsp chopped parsley
5 ml/1 tsp chopped fresh mixed herbs
grated rind of ½ lemon
salt and pepper
1 egg, beaten

Melt the butter or margarine in a small saucepan and stir in the breadcrumbs, nutmeg, herbs and lemon rind. Add salt and pepper to taste. Stir in enough of the beaten egg to bind the mixture.

SUFFICIENT FOR 1 (1.5–2 KG/ 3¼–4½ LB) CHICKEN, A BONED JOINT OF VEAL OR 8 (75 G/3 OZ) FISH FILLETS

> **MRS BEETON'S TIP** A bird, joint of meat or fish should always be stuffed just before being cooked. If preferred, the stuffing may be shaped into 12 or 16 small balls and baked in a preheated 180°C/350°F/gas 4 oven for 15–20 minutes.

CHESTNUT AND ONION STUFFING

Use double the quantity listed below when stuffing the neck end of a 5–6 kg/11–13 lb turkey.

1 large onion, thickly sliced
125 ml/4 fl oz chicken stock or water
450 g/1 lb chestnuts, prepared and
    cooked (see Mrs Beeton's Tip) or
300 g/11 oz canned chestnuts
salt and pepper
1 egg, beaten

Combine the onion and stock or water in a small saucepan. Bring the liquid to the boil, lower the heat and simmer for about 10 minutes until the onion is tender; drain and chop finely.

Meanwhile mince the chestnuts or chop them finely. Combine the chestnuts and onion in a bowl, stir in salt and pepper to taste and add enough of the egg to bind the stuffing.

SUFFICIENT FOR A 2.5 KG/5½ LB DUCK

> **MRS BEETON'S TIP** To prepare chestnuts, make a slit in the rounded side of each nut, then bake them at 180°C/ 350°F/gas 4 for 30 minutes or cook them in boiling water for 20 minutes. Remove the shells and skins while still hot. Put the shelled nuts in a saucepan with just enough stock to cover. Bring the liquid to the boil, lower the heat and simmer for 45–60 minutes or until tender.

APRICOT STUFFING

This stuffing is particularly good with pork, but may also be used with lamb, any poultry or game birds. Use double the quantity listed below when stuffing a 4–5 kg/9–11 lb goose.

75 g/3 oz dried apricots, soaked overnight
    in water to cover
75 g/3 oz soft white or Granary
    breadcrumbs
25 g/1 oz butter, melted
1.25 ml/¼ tsp salt
1.25 ml/¼ tsp freshly ground black
    pepper
pinch each of dried thyme, ground mace
    and grated nutmeg
1 celery stick, finely chopped

Drain the apricots, reserving the liquid, and chop finely. Put in a bowl with the breadcrumbs, butter, salt, pepper, thyme and spices. Stir in the celery and moisten the mixture with a little of the reserved apricot liquid.

SUFFICIENT FOR A BONED JOINT OF PORK OR 1 (2.5 KG/5½ LB) DUCK

MRS BEETON'S TIP Ready-to-eat dried apricots may be used for this stuffing, in which case the mixture should be moistened with a little vegetable or chicken stock.

PRUNE AND APPLE STUFFING

Use double the quantity listed below when stuffing a 4–5 kg/9–11 lb goose.

100 g/4 oz prunes, soaked overnight and
    drained
1 large cooking apple
100 g/4 oz boiled long-grain white or
    brown rice
50 g/2 oz flaked almonds
50 g/2 oz butter, softened
salt and pepper
grated rind and juice of ½ lemon
1 egg, beaten

Stone and chop the prunes. Peel, core and roughly chop the apple. Combine the chopped fruits in a bowl with the rice, almonds and butter. Add salt and pepper to taste and stir in the lemon rind and juice. Add enough of the beaten egg to moisten the stuffing.

SUFFICIENT FOR A BONED JOINT OF PORK OR 1 (2.5 KG/5½ LB) DUCK

MRS BEETON'S TIP Canned prunes may be used for this stuffing. Choose the variety canned in natural juice and substitute a little of the juice for half the lemon juice in the recipe above.

CARAMEL SAUCE

200 g/7 oz caster sugar
30 ml/2 tbsp chilled orange juice
15 ml/1 tbsp orange-flavoured liqueur
    (optional)

Put the sugar in a heavy bottomed saucepan. Add 125 ml/4 fl oz water and stir over low heat for 3–4 minutes until the sugar has dissolved. Increase the heat and boil, without stirring, until the syrup turns a light golden brown colour. Do not allow it to darken too much or it will taste bitter.

Immediately plunge the bottom of the saucepan into warm water to arrest further cooking. Allow the caramel mixture to cool slightly, then carefully add a further 75 ml/ 3 fl oz water and the orange juice. Return the saucepan to a low heat and stir constantly until the mixture becomes smooth. Remove from the heat, cool slightly, then stir in the liqueur, if using.

SERVES 4

MRS BEETON'S TIP Caramel sauce keeps well in a covered jar in the refrigerator. Allow the sauce to cool completely before pouring it into the jar. It will keep for at least 6 months.

CHOCOLATE SAUCE

75 g/3 oz caster sugar
10 ml/2 tsp cornflour
300 ml/½ pint milk
50 g/2 oz plain chocolate, broken into
    chunks
25 g/1 oz butter

Combine the sugar and cornflour in a saucepan. Stir in a little of the milk to make a paste, then stir in the rest of the milk.

Heat gently, stirring all the time, until the sugar has dissolved, then bring to the boil. Cook for 2 minutes, stirring occasionally.

Remove from the heat, then stir in the chocolate and butter until smooth and creamy.

MAKES ABOUT 300 ML/½ PINT

☆ **FREEZING TIP** Cover the surface of the sauce with a piece of dampened greaseproof paper to prevent a skin forming. Cool the sauce quickly by plunging the bottom of the saucepan into a large bowl of ice cold water. Freeze for up to 3 months.

BRANDY BUTTER

50 g/2 oz butter
100 g/4 oz caster sugar
15–30 ml/1–2 tbsp brandy

In a bowl, cream the butter until soft. Gradually beat in the sugar until the mixture is pale and light. Work in the brandy, a little at a time, taking care not to allow the mixture to curdle. Chill before using. If the mixture has separated slightly after standing, beat well before serving.

MAKES ABOUT 150 G/5 OZ

VARIATIONS

SHERRY BUTTER Make as for Brandy Butter but substitute sherry for the brandy. Add a stiffly beaten egg white, if a softer texture is preferred.
VANILLA BUTTER Make as for Brandy Butter but substitute 5 ml/1 tsp vanilla essence for the brandy.
ORANGE OR LEMON BUTTER Cream the grated rind of 1 orange or ½ lemon with the butter and sugar, then gradually beat in 15 ml/1 tbsp orange juice or 5 ml/1 tsp lemon juice. Omit the brandy.

DRINKS

From nostalgic images of lemonade on the lawn to heady sips
of sloe gin, this brief chapter provides all the information
needed to conjure up the right drink for the occasion.

Home brewing is a separate subject, re-
quiring attention beyond the scope of this
book. These recipes are for refreshing
drinks that may be prepared and chilled for
several days or frozen for a few months. A
couple of heartwarming recipes of different
types are also included, including a beef
tea which should be served within a day or
so when fresh or frozen for future use.

STORING HOME-MADE DRINKS

The majority of the drinks should be used
within 3–5 days of being made. In summer,
make a double quantity of lemonade or
other soft drink to keep covered in the
refrigerator – it will be appreciated by
those drivers avoiding alcohol as well as
youngsters. Or simply serve a cold drink
instead of tea.

Concentrated fruit drinks will not keep
for long periods unless they are correctly
bottled and processed as for bottled fruit.
This time-consuming task can be avoided
by freezing the drink instead. Freeze in ice
cube trays until firm, then transfer to bags.
When added to mineral water, a few cubes
of the drink will thaw quickly.

Savoury beverages, such as beef tea, may
be reduced to a concentrate before freezing; when required, they can be quickly
thawed by adding the required volume of
hot water and heating gently. Remember
to note the extent to which the drink
was reduced on the pack label – this way
you know how much water to add when
reheating it.

SERVING DRINKS

If you have gone to the trouble of preparing
a special drink, it is certainly worth the
effort of adding a few finishing touches
when serving it. Chilling glasses in the
refrigerator for 30 minutes before serving a
cold drink is a professional touch; always
remember to add ice to cold drinks. Here
are some additional suggestions:

■ Add sprigs of mint or lemon balm
to iced teas or fruit drinks.

■ Cut thin slices of lemon, orange or
lime to decorate fruit drinks.

■ In summer, strawberries and
wafer-thin slices of cucumber combine
well in light fruit drinks.

■ Make a light alcoholic punch by
combining equal quantities of dry
white wine and diluted Elderflower
Cordial (page 65) or Lemonade (page
64).

■ To frost the rims of glasses, dip
them first in a little water or lemon
juice, then in sugar. Add pink or green
food colouring to the water for a pretty
effect.

■ When serving hot drinks such as
beef tea, remember to warm glasses
first or put a spoon in each glass before
pouring in the hot liquid.

dissolve the sugar, until boiling. Leave over low heat for 30 minutes, then set aside until cold.

Add the orange juice, stir and strain into a clean jug. Squeeze, then discard the lemon wedges. Crush the Campden tablet in a mug and add a little boiling water. Stir until dissolved, then add to the squash. Stir well before pouring into a bottle. Cover and store in the refrigerator for up to 3 weeks. To serve, dilute to taste with water, soda water or mineral water.

MAKES ABOUT 1 LITRE/1¾ PINTS

ORANGE SQUASH

Illustrated on page 73

Campden tablets, available from chemists and shops specialising in wine-making equipment, consist of sodium metabisulphite. They are used for killing off wild yeasts in fruit when making wine. Adding a Campden tablet to this squash helps to prevent the juice from fermenting.

grated rind of 3 oranges
450 g/l lb sugar
¼ lemon, cut in wedges
300 ml/½ pint fresh orange juice
1 Campden tablet

Combine the orange rind, sugar and lemon wedges in a saucepan. Add 450 ml/ ¾ pint water and heat gently, stirring to

BARLEY WATER

Illustrated on page 73

This makes a nutritious drink, which keeps well in the refrigerator. If the lemon juice is omitted, it may be stirred into milk.

25 g/l oz pearl barley
grated rind of 1 lemon
125 ml/4 fl oz lemon juice
sugar to taste

Put the pearl barley in a saucepan with water to cover. Bring to the boil and boil for 2 minutes, then strain into a clean pan. Stir in the lemon rind, juice and 1.1 litres/2 pints water. Heat gently, stirring occasionally, until boiling. Reduce the heat, cover the pan and cook gently for 45 minutes. Leave, covered, until cold.

Strain, sweeten to taste, then store in a covered container in the refrigerator for up to 1 week. Alternatively, freeze in ice cube trays or small containers.

MAKES ABOUT 1.2 LITRES/2¼ PINTS

LEMONADE

Illustrated on page 73

A jug of refreshing iced lemonade is the perfect cooler for a hot summer's day.

1.8 kg/4 lb sugar
grated rind of 2 lemons
1 litre/1¾ pints lemon juice

Put the sugar in a saucepan with 1 litre/ 1¾ pints water. Heat gently, stirring until all the sugar has dissolved, then stir in the lemon rind. Boil for 5 minutes without further stirring. Allow to cool.

Stir in the lemon juice, strain into clean jugs or bottles and store in the refrigerator. Dilute with iced water to serve.

MAKES ABOUT 3 LITRES/5¼ PINTS

GINGER BEER

As anyone who has ever experienced the explosion caused by unwisely stored ginger beer will know, fermentation causes strong pressure inside bottles. It is therefore important to use sturdy, properly sterilized beer bottles with clip-on bottle seals or screw tops. Store in a cardboard box in a cool dark place, preferably on a concrete floor.

25 g/1 oz fresh root ginger, bruised
thinly pared rind and juice of 2 lemons
450 g/1 lb sugar
7.5 ml/1½ tsp cream of tartar
1 sachet dried beer yeast

Combine the ginger, lemon rind, sugar and cream of tartar in a suitable white brewing bucket with lid. Add 5 litres/8¾ pints hot water. Stir gently until the sugar has dissolved, then leave to cool.

Add the lemon juice to the cooled liquid and sprinkle the yeast over the surface. Cover and leave in a warm place for 48 hours, skimming off the yeast head after 24 hours. When fermentation has finished, skim again before bottling.

Thoroughly wash sufficient beer bottles to hold the ginger beer, and sterilize them in Campden solution (see Mrs Beeton's Tip) or by using another suitable wine-making product. Siphon the ginger beer into the bottles, being careful not to disturb the deposit in the bottom of the container. Seal the bottles tightly and leave in a warm place for 3 days. Use at once or store in a cool dark place until required, checking the bottles frequently.

MAKES ABOUT 5.25 LITRES/9¼ PINTS

MRS BEETON'S TIP Use proper beer bottles as mineral bottles may not be strong enough to withstand the pressures. Wash them thoroughly inside and out, then sterilize them and the closures in a solution of 2 crushed Campden tablets and 2.5 ml/½ tsp citric acid in 500 ml/18 fl oz water.

SPARKLING MINT TEA

Illustrated on page 73

20 ml/4 tsp tea leaves
75 g/3 oz caster sugar
12 mint leaves
300 ml/½ pint soda water or sparkling
   mineral water
ice cubes
4 lemon slices

Put the tea leaves into a large heatproof jug and add 600 ml/1 pint boiling water.

Infuse for 3–7 minutes. Strain into a clean jug and stir in the sugar and 4 mint leaves. Allow to cool. The tea may be covered and kept in the refrigerator for up to 2 days. Alternatively, it may be frozen in ice cube trays.

Stir in the soda or sparkling mineral water and pour into 4 tall glasses. Add ice cubes, 1 lemon slice and 2 mint leaves to each glass. Stir, then serve at once.

SERVES 4

———————— ◇ ————————

ELDERFLOWER CORDIAL

Diluted with plenty of iced water, this makes a refreshing drink. Small quantities may also be used to flavour stewed fruit such as gooseberries or greengages.

900 g/2 lb caster sugar
30 g/1¼ oz citric acid
1 lemon
10 elderflower heads, washed and
   drained

Put the sugar in a large heatproof bowl. Add 600 ml/1 pint boiling water and stir until all the sugar has dissolved. Stir in the citric acid.

Grate the lemon and add the rind to the bowl, then slice the fruit. Add the lemon slices to the bowl with the elderflower heads. Cover and allow to stand for 12 hours or overnight. Strain through muslin, bottle and store for 1 month before serving.

MAKES ABOUT 600 ML/1 PINT

SLOE GIN

450 g/1 lb ripe sloes
225 g/8 oz caster sugar
1 litre/1¾ pints dry gin

Remove stalks and leaves from the sloes, then wash and prick them all over. Put them in a jar which can be fitted with an airtight seal.

In a large jug or bowl, dissolve the sugar in the gin and pour it on to the sloes. Cover the jar and store it in a cool dark place for 3 months, giving it a gentle shake every few days to extract and distribute the fruit flavour. Strain, bottle and store for 3 months more before serving.

MAKES ABOUT 1.25 LITRES/2¼ PINTS

BEEF TEA

Beef tea freezes very well and thaws quickly if frozen in ice cube trays.

400 g/14 oz shin, flank or skirt of beef
2.5 ml/½ tsp salt

Set the oven at 140°C/275°F/gas 1. Trim off all visible fat from the meat; cut it into 2.5 cm/1 inch cubes, then put it in a casserole. Add 500 ml/18 fl oz water and the salt. Cover and cook for 4 hours.

Strain the liquid through a fine sieve lined with scalded muslin into a clean bowl. Allow to cool, then chill the beef tea and skim off any fat. Reheat, without boiling, taste for seasoning and serve as a light soup or beverage.

SERVES 2

CANDIED FRUITS AND CONFECTIONERY

Home-candied fruit, hand-made sweets and filled chocolates make highly acceptable gifts and are the ultimate dinner-party sweetmeat. This comprehensive chapter includes instructions for making all these, some simple, others more difficult, to suit your ability and the time you want to spend on creating confectionery.

With good basic equipment, plenty of time, patience and enthusiasm, skills such as working with sugar or tempering chocolate can readily be mastered.

EQUIPMENT

A stainless steel or other high-quality saucepan and sugar thermometer are the first items you need. A marble board and large palette knife are best for working boiled sugar syrup, although a plain white (fairly heavy) enamelled tray may be used instead. Some work surfaces withstand the heat of the boiled sugar: others do not. Marble gives the best results.

Chocolate Work Depending on the type of chocolates you hope to make, you may need moulds and/or a dipping fork (a fine, two-pronged fork). To pipe detail on the set chocolates you will need small greaseproof paper piping bags and a small, plain piping tube (from suppliers of cake decorating materials).

SIMPLE TESTS FOR SUGAR BOILING

A sugar thermometer takes the guess-work out of sweet-making, but syrup can be boiled without stirring and the temperature gauged approximately by using the following tests:

Thread Stage (105°C/220°F) Test by dipping a spoon in the syrup and then pressing another spoon on to the back of it and pulling away. If a thread forms, the syrup is ready.

Blow Stage (110°C/225°F) Test by dipping the top of a metal skewer in the syrup, draining it over the saucepan and then blowing through the hole. A small bubble should form which floats in the air for a second.

Soft Ball Stage (115°C/235°F) Test by dropping about 2.5 ml/½ tsp of the syrup into a bowl of iced water. You should be able to mould the syrup between your fingers to make a soft ball.

Hard Ball Stage (120°C/250°F) Test as for soft ball, but boil for 2–3 minutes longer. A larger, harder ball should be formed.

Small Crack Stage (140°C/275°F) Test by adding a few drops of the mixture to a bowl of iced water. The mixture should become brittle; a thin piece should snap.

Large Crack Stage (155°C/310°F) Test as for small crack, but boil for 2–3 minutes longer. The syrup will be very brittle and will not stick to the teeth when bitten.

CANDIED AND CRYSTALLIZED FRUIT

Shop-bought candied fruit is a succulent and expensive luxury but it can be made at home without great skill or special equipment. The main requirement is patience as the process takes about 15 minutes a day for 10–14 days. Any attempt to increase the strength of the syrup too quickly will result in tough, hardened, and shrivelled fruit. Sugar alone can be used for syrup making but the fruit's texture is better if part of the sugar is replaced by glucose. Powdered glucose weighs the same as sugar, but if using liquid glucose, increase the weight by one-fifth.

Use well-flavoured fruits, fresh or canned, for example apricots, pineapple or large, juicy plums. Very soft fruits, such as raspberries, tend to disintegrate. Fresh fruit should be firm yet ripe. Good quality canned fruit can be used; it lacks some of the full fresh flavour, but the canning process gives a good texture for candying. Canned fruit does not require cooking and the process is quicker than for fresh fruit.

Processed fruit should be packed in waxed-paper lined cardboard boxes. Interleave layers of fruit with waxed paper. Store in a cool, *dry* place: well processed fruit will keep for several months.

FRESH FRUIT

Day 1 Prepare the fruit according to type, discarding stones and cores or peel. Prick small crab-apples, apricots, fleshy plums or greengages several times to the centre with a stainless steel fork.

Cover the prepared fruit with boiling water and simmer gently until just tender, 10–15 minutes for firm fruits, only 3–4 minutes for tender fruits. Overcooking at this stage makes the fruit squashy, while undercooking makes it dark and tough.

For each 450 g/1 lb fruit, make a syrup from 250 ml/8 fl oz poaching water, 50 g/ 2 oz sugar and 100 g/4 oz glucose. Alternatively, use 150 g/5 oz preserving sugar instead of sugar and glucose. Stir until the sugar has dissolved, then bring to the boil.

Drain the fruit and place it in a small bowl, then pour the boiling syrup over it. If there is not enough syrup to cover it, make up some more, using the same proportions. Cover with a plate to keep the fruit under the syrup and leave for 24 hours.

Day 2 Drain the syrup into a saucepan. Add 50 g/2 oz sugar for each original 250 ml/ 8 fl oz water. Bring to the boil, then pour the syrup over the fruit. Cover and leave as before.

Days 3–7 Repeat Day 2.

Day 8 Add 75 g/3 oz sugar for every original 250 ml/8 fl oz water, heat and stir until dissolved. Add the drained fruit and boil for 3–4 minutes, then pour fruit and syrup back into the bowl. This boiling makes the fruit plump. Leave for 48 hours.

Day 10 Repeat Day 8. When cooled, the resulting syrup should be of the consistency of fairly thick honey. If the syrup is still thin, repeat Day 8 again. Leave for 4 days.

Day 14 The fruit will keep in this heavy syrup for 2–3 weeks or for 2 months in a covered jar in the refrigerator. To complete the process, remove the fruit from the syrup. *Do not pierce the fruit.* Place it on a wire rack over a plate and allow to drain for a few minutes.

Put the rack into a very cool oven (not higher than 50°C/122°F). Use an oven thermometer to check the temperature and wedge the door ajar to prevent the temperature from increasing.

Candied fruit caramelizes easily and the flavour is then spoilt. Drying should take 3–6 hours if the heat is continuous; it may take 2–3 days if using residual heat on several occasions. Do not allow the metal rack to touch the hot sides of the oven as this will cause the wire to become too hot. Turn the fruit gently with a fork, until it is no longer sticky to handle.

Pack in cardboard boxes with waxed paper lining the box and separating the layers. Store in a dry, cool place and do not keep for many months as the succulence will be lost.

Candied fruit should have a dry surface. If it remains sticky, the final sugar concentration in the fruit is probably too low. Humid storage conditions should be avoided.

MRS BEETON'S TIP If you are candying several fruits at the same time, use separate syrups. Use surplus syrup for fruit salads, stewed fruit or sweetening puddings.

CANNED FRUIT

Try pineapple rings or cubes, plums, peaches or halved apricots. Keep the sizes as uniform as possible. These quantities are for about 450 g/1 lb drained fruit.

Day 1 Put the drained fruit into a large bowl. Measure the syrup into a pan and make it up to 250 ml/8 fl oz with water if necessary. Add 200 g/7 oz sugar or 100 g/4 oz sugar and 100 g/4 oz glucose. Heat gently and stir until the sugar has dissolved. Bring to the boil, then pour the syrup over the fruit. If there is not enough syrup to cover the fruit, prepare some more by using 225 g/8 oz sugar to 200 ml/7 fl oz water. Keep the fruit under the syrup with a plate. Leave for 24 hours.

Day 2 Drain the fruit, dissolve 50 g/2 oz sugar in the syrup, bring to the boil and pour over the fruit. Leave for 24 hours.

Days 3–4 Repeat Day 2.

Day 5 Pour the syrup into a saucepan. Add 75 g/3 oz sugar, warm the syrup to dissolve the sugar, then add the fruit. Boil for 3–4 minutes. Replace in the bowl. Leave for 48 hours.

Day 7 Repeat Day 5 and let the fruit boil until a little syrup cooled on a plate has the consistency of thick honey. Leave to soak for 3–4 days. If the syrup seems thin, add a further 75 g/3 oz sugar, dissolve it and boil the syrup with the fruit for a further few minutes. Leave to soak for 3–4 days.

Day 11 Finish the fruit as when candying fresh fruit (Day 14).

CANDIED ANGELICA

Pick bright, tender stalks in April, cut off the root ends and leaves. Make a brine with 15 g/½ oz salt in 2 litres/3½ pints water, bring it to the boil. Soak the stalks in brine for 10 minutes. Rinse in cold water. Put in a pan of fresh boiling water and boil for 5–7 minutes. Drain. Scrape to remove the outer skin. Continue as for candying fresh fruit from Day 1.

CANDIED PEEL

Use oranges, lemons or grapefruit. Scrub the fruit thoroughly. Halve and remove the pulp carefully to avoid damaging the peel. Boil the peel for 1 hour. Give grapefruit peel, which is bitter, several changes of water. Drain, and continue as for candying fresh fruit from Day 1. It is customary to pour some glacé syrup into half peels to set.

CRYSTALLIZING FRUIT

Have some granulated sugar on a sheet of polythene, greaseproof paper or foil. Lift a piece of fruit on a fork, dip it quickly into *boiling* water, drain briefly, then roll it in the sugar until evenly coated.

Hummus and Felafel (both on page 49)

Spaghetti alla Carbonara (page 50) garnished with basil, and Pasta, Anchovy and Sweetcorn Salad (page 52)

Clockwise from bottom: **Chiffonade Dressing served with avocado, Claret Dressing and French Dressing (all on page 57), Stone Fruit Vinegar (page 139) and Raspberry Vinegar (page 138)**

Pesto Genovese garnished with pine nuts and basil, and Tuna Sauce served with eggs and garnished with capers and lemon (both on page 58)

Clockwise from bottom: **Sparkling Mint Tea** (page 64), **Lemonade** (page 64), **Orange Squash in bottle and glass, and Barley Water** (both on page 63)

74

Clockwise from top: Creamy Fudge (page 82), Peanut Brittle (page 80), Buttered Brazils (page 83) and Butterscotch (page 80); *Centre:* Mint Humbugs (page 87)

75

Coconut Ice and Turkish Delight (both on page 85) and Nougat (page 86)

Fondant Sweets and Hand-made Chocolates (page 91)

MAKING A GLACÉ FINISH

This gives a smooth, shiny finish. Over gentle heat, dissolve 450 g/1 lb granulated sugar in 150 ml/¼ pint water, then boil. Dip each fruit into boiling water for 20 seconds, then drain. Pour a little boiling syrup into a warm cup, quickly dip the fruit and place it on a wire rack. When all the fruit has been dipped, place the rack in a temperature not exceeding 50°C/122°F, and turn the fruit often to ensure even drying.

When the syrup in the small cup becomes cloudy, it must be discarded and replaced from the saucepan, which must be kept hot (but not boiling) and closely covered.

QUICK CANDIED PEEL

Soak grapefruit or lemon peel overnight to extract some of the bitterness. Cut the peel into long strips, 5 mm/¼ inch wide. Put in a saucepan, cover with cold water and bring slowly to the boil. Drain, add fresh water and bring to the boil again. Drain, and repeat 3 more times. Weigh the cooled peel and place with an equal quantity of sugar in a pan. Just cover with boiling water, and boil gently until the peel is tender and clear. Cool, strain from the syrup, and toss the peel in fine granulated sugar on grease-proof paper. Spread out on a wire rack to dry for several hours. Roll again in sugar if at all sticky. When quite dry, store in covered jars. Use within 3–4 months.

PULLING SUGAR

In some sweet recipes the boiled sugar mixture is pulled while still warm and pliable to give it a satiny, shiny look. The technique is similar to that employed when making barley sugar. When the syrup has reached the correct temperature, pour it on to an oiled, heat-resistant surface. Allow it to settle for a few minutes until a skin has formed, then using two oiled palette knives, turn the mixture sides to the centre until it cools enough to handle. Oil your hands as a protective measure, then carefully pull the syrup into a sausage shape, working quickly. Fold in the ends, twist and pull again. Repeat the pulling until the candy has a shiny surface. When it is beginning to harden, shape it into a long rope as thick as is needed, and cut quickly into small pieces with oiled scissors. If all the mixture cannot be pulled at once, leave it on an oiled baking sheet in a warm place to keep it soft.

Several colours can be introduced by dividing the hot syrup into different portions before cooling, and introducing a few drops of food colouring to each. Pull these separately, then lay them together for the final pulling and shaping. One portion may be left unpulled and clear and added at the final shaping stage.

SIMPLE TOFFEE

oil for greasing
400 g/14 oz lump sugar
pinch of cream of tartar

Grease a 15 cm/6 inch square baking tin. Put the sugar into a saucepan, add 125 ml/4 fl oz water and heat gently, stirring, until all the sugar has dissolved. Bring to the boil, add the cream of tartar and boil without stirring until the syrup registers 140°C/275°F on a sugar thermometer, the small crack stage (see page 66).

When ready, pour the syrup into the prepared tin, leave to cool, then score the surface deeply with a knife, marking it into squares. When set, break into squares as marked, wrap in waxed paper and store in an airtight tin.

MAKES ABOUT 400 G/14 OZ

VARIATIONS

NUT TOFFEE Add 75 g/3 oz flaked almonds or chopped walnuts with the sugar and sugar.
GINGER TOFFEE Add 2.5 ml/½ tsp ground ginger with the water.
VANILLA TOFFEE Add 2.5 ml/½ tsp vanilla essence with the cream of tartar.

BARLEY SUGAR

oil for greasing
30 ml/2 tbsp pearl barley
450 g/1 lb lump sugar
juice of ½ lemon
pinch of cream of tartar

Put the barley in a saucepan with 300 ml/½ pint cold water. Bring to the boil, drain and rinse the barley under cold water. Return it to the clean pan and add 1 litre/1¾ pints cold water. Bring to the boil, lower the heat and simmer, covered, for about 1¾ hours.

Strain the mixture into a measuring jug. Make up to 500 ml/18 fl oz with cold water. Put the sugar in a heavy-bottomed saucepan with the barley water. Stir over low heat for 3–4 minutes until the sugar has dissolved. Increase the heat and boil, without stirring, until the syrup registers 115°C/235°F on a sugar thermometer, the soft ball stage (see page 66).

Add the lemon juice and continue boiling until the syrup reaches 155°C/310°F, the large crack stage (see page 66).

Pour the mixture on to a lightly oiled slab or large flat laminated board. Allow to cool for a few minutes, then fold the sides to the centre, using an oiled palette knife. Cut into strips with oiled scissors, and twist each strip. When cold and set, store in an airtight jar.

MAKES ABOUT 375 G/13 OZ

EVERTON TOFFEE

oil for greasing
200 g/7 oz granulated sugar
75 g/3 oz soft light brown sugar
pinch of cream of tartar
10 ml/2 tsp lemon juice
50 g/2 oz butter

Grease a 20 cm/8 inch square baking tin. Combine the sugars in a saucepan, add 175 ml/6 fl oz water and heat gently, stirring, until all the sugar has dissolved. Bring to the boil, add the cream of tartar and boil without stirring until the syrup registers 140°C/275°F on a sugar thermometer, the small crack stage (see page 66). Add the lemon juice and butter and continue boiling without stirring until the syrup reaches 155°C/310°F, the large crack stage (see page 66).

Pour the mixture immediately into the prepared tin. When beginning to set score the surface deeply with a knife, marking it into squares. When set, break into squares as marked, wrap in waxed paper and store in an airtight tin.

MAKES ABOUT 350 G/12 OZ

> ☕ **MRS BEETON'S TIP** When buying a sugar thermometer, look for one with a movable clip that fits on the side of the saucepan. Test it after purchase by putting it in a saucepan of cold water and heating slowly to boiling point. Check that it reads 100°C/220°F. Allow it to cool in the water. Always warm the thermometer in a jug of warm water before using it to test boiling syrup, returning it to the jug of water after use.

RUSSIAN TOFFEE

oil for greasing
400 g/14 oz sugar
200 g/7 oz redcurrant jelly
100 g/4 oz butter
125 ml/4 fl oz single cream
pinch of cream of tartar
2.5 ml/½ tsp vanilla essence

Grease a 20 cm/8 inch square baking tin. Combine the sugar, redcurrant jelly, butter and cream in a saucepan. Heat gently, stir-

ring, until all the sugar has dissolved. Add the cream of tartar and bring to the boil, stirring frequently. Boil without stirring until the mixture registers 120°C/250°F on a sugar thermomenter, the hard ball stage (see page 66).

Pour immediately into the prepared tin and score the surface deeply with a knife, marking it into squares. When set, separate into squares as marked, wrap in waxed paper and store in an airtight tin.

MAKES ABOUT 675 G/1½ LB

TREACLE TOFFEE

oil for greasing
100 g/4 oz butter
100 g/4 oz black treacle
150 g/5 oz soft dark brown sugar
pinch of cream of tartar

Grease a 15 cm/6 inch square baking tin. Combine the butter, treacle and sugar in a heavy bottomed saucepan and add 30 ml/2 tbsp water. Heat gently, stirring, until the sugar has dissolved.

Add the cream of tartar, bring to the boil and boil without stirring until the mixture registers 120°C/250°F on a sugar thermometer, the hard ball stage (see page 66).

Pour immediately into the prepared tin and score the surface deeply with a knife, marking it into squares. When set, break into squares as marked, wrap in waxed paper and store in an airtight tin.

MAKES ABOUT 300 G/11 OZ

PEANUT BRITTLE

Illustrated on page 74

oil for greasing
300 g/11 oz unsalted peanuts
350 g/12 oz granulated sugar
150 g/5 oz soft light brown sugar
150 g/5 oz golden syrup
50 g/2 oz butter
1.25 ml/¼ tsp bicarbonate of soda

Grease a 20 cm/8 inch square baking tin. Spread out the nuts on a baking sheet and warm them very gently in a 150°C/300°F/ gas 2 oven. Meanwhile combine the sugars, golden syrup and 125 ml/4 fl oz water in a heavy-bottomed saucepan and heat gently, stirring, until all the sugar has dissolved.

Add the butter, bring to the boil and boil gently without stirring until the syrup registers 155°C/310°F on a sugar thermometer, the large crack stage (see page 66). Stir in the bicarbonate of soda and the warmed nuts.

Pour the mixture into the prepared tin. When almost set, score the surface deeply with a knife, marking it into bars. When set, break as marked, wrap in waxed paper and store in an airtight tin.

MAKES ABOUT 1 KG/2¼ LB

> **MRS BEETON'S TIP** Use a strong, heavy-bottomed saucepan for sweet-making, to prevent mixtures sticking and burning. Syrups and sugar-based mixtures tend to rise very quickly during cooking, so make sure you use a large enough pan.

BUTTERSCOTCH

Illustrated on page 74

oil for greasing
100 g/4 oz caster sugar
100 g/4 oz butter
75 ml/3 fl oz liquid glucose
125 ml/4 fl oz single cream

Grease an 18 cm/7 inch square baking tin. Combine all the ingredients in a large heavy-bottomed saucepan. Heat them very gently, stirring, until all the sugar has dissolved. Bring to the boil and boil without stirring until the mixture registers 140°C/ 275°F on a sugar thermometer, the small crack stage (see page 66).

Pour the mixture immediately into the prepared tin. When beginning to set, score the surface deeply with a knife, marking it into squares. When set, break into squares as marked, wrap in waxed paper and store in an airtight tin.

MAKES ABOUT 225 G/8 OZ

> **MRS BEETON'S TIP** For a special gift, overwrap each piece of butterscotch in brightly coloured cellophane paper, twist the ends and pack in a decorative box or tin.

CREAM CARAMELS

oil for greasing
200 g/7 oz sugar
200 g/7 oz golden syrup
125 ml/4 fl oz evaporated milk
2.5 ml½ tsp vanilla essence

Grease a 20 cm/8 inch square baking tin. Combine all the ingredients except the vanilla essence in a heavy-bottomed saucepan. Heat gently, stirring, until the sugar has dissolved. Bring to the boil and boil without stirring until the mixture registers 120°C/250°F on a sugar thermometer, the hard ball stage (see page 66).

Stir in the vanilla essence and pour the mixture into the prepared tin. When the caramel is cold, score the surface deeply with a knife, marking it into squares. When set, cut into squares as marked, wrap in waxed paper and store in an airtight tin.

MAKES ABOUT 400 G/14 OZ

CHOCOLATE CARAMELS

oil for greasing
150 g/5 oz caster sugar
15 ml/1 tbsp drinking chocolate powder
75 ml/5 tbsp milk
15 ml/1 tbsp liquid glucose
100 g/4 oz butter
75 g/5 tbsp single cream
2.5 ml/½ tsp vanilla essence

Grease an 18 cm/7 inch square baking tin. Combine the sugar, chocolate powder, milk and glucose in a heavy-bottomed saucepan. Add one third of the butter and heat gently, stirring until all the sugar has dissolved.

Bring the mixture rapidly to the boil, stirring to prevent burning, and boil until the mixture registers 110°C/225°F on a sugar thermometer, the blow stage (see page 66).

Stir in half the remaining butter and boil for 5 minutes more or until the mixture registers 112°C/230°F. Remove the pan from the heat and quickly stir in the remaining butter, with the cream and vanilla essence.

Return the pan to the heat. Stirring constantly, boil the mixture until it registers 115°C/235°F, the soft ball stage (see page 66). Pour into the prepared tin. When beginning to set, score the surface deeply with a knife, marking it into squares. When set, cut into squares as marked.

MAKES ABOUT 300 G/11 OZ

> 🍲 **MRS BEETON'S TIP** Grated chocolate may be used instead of the drinking chocolate powder, if preferred. You will need about 75 g/3 oz.

CREAMY FUDGE

Illustrated on page 74

oil for greasing
400 g/14 oz sugar
125 ml/4 fl oz milk
50 g/2 oz butter
2.5 ml/½ tsp vanilla essence

Grease an 18 cm/7 inch square baking tin. Combine all the ingredients except the vanilla essence in a large saucepan. Heat gently until the sugar has dissolved, then bring to the boil.

Boil, stirring constantly, until the mixture registers 115°C/235°F on a sugar thermometer, the soft ball stage (see page 66). Remove the pan from the heat and stir in the vanilla essence. Cool for 2 minutes, then beat the mixture until it becomes thick and creamy.

Pour into the prepared tin. When nearly set, score the surface of the fudge deeply with a knife, marking it into squares. When set, cut into squares as marked and store in an airtight tin lined with waxed paper.

MAKES ABOUT 450 G/1 LB

MRS BEETON'S TIP Fudge crystallizes if the sugar is not dissolved properly and if crystals are allowed to form on the sides of the saucepan. To prevent this happening, either grease the saucepan lightly with a little of the butter used in the recipe or cover the saucepan with a lid when the mixture comes to the boil. The steam will wash down the sides of the pan. Remove the lid after 2–3 minutes and boil without stirring until the soft ball stage is reached. The crystals may also be brushed down from the sides of the pan into the mixture, using a clean brush dipped in cold water.

CHOCOLATE FUDGE

oil for greasing
400 g/14 oz sugar
50 g/2 oz golden syrup
50 g/2 oz butter
25 g/1 oz cocoa
75 ml/5 tbsp milk
45 ml/3 tbsp single cream

Grease a 15 cm/6 inch square cake tin. Combine all the ingredients in a heavy-bottomed saucepan and heat gently until all the sugar has dissolved. Bring to the boil.

Boil, stirring constantly, until the mixture registers 115°C/235°F on a sugar thermometer, the soft ball stage (see page 66). Cool for 5 minutes, then beat the fudge until creamy and matt in appearance.

Pour the fudge into the prepared tin. Leave until cold before cutting into squares. Store in an airtight tin lined with waxed paper.

MAKES ABOUT 450 G/1 LB

VARIATION

CHOCOLATE NUT FUDGE Stir in 100 g/4 oz chopped walnuts or almonds during the final beating.

MRS BEETON'S TIP It is important to observe the short cooling time before beating fudge, but the mixture must not overcool or it will be difficult to pour it into the prepared tin.

BUTTERED ALMONDS, WALNUTS OR BRAZILS

Illustrated on page 74

Brown, buttery and practically irresistible, buttered nuts make a most acceptable gift. Set each one in an individual fluted paper case and pack in a pretty box or tin.

oil for greasing
50 g/2 oz blanched almonds, halved
   walnuts or whole Brazil nuts
200 g/7 oz demerara sugar
10 ml/2 tsp liquid glucose
pinch of cream of tartar
50 g/2 oz butter

Spread out the nuts on an oiled baking sheet and warm them very gently in a 150°C/300°F/gas 2 oven. Put the sugar into a saucepan, add 90 ml/6 tbsp water and heat gently, stirring, until the sugar has dissolved.

Bring the mixture to the boil. Add the glucose, cream of tartar and butter. When the butter has dissolved, boil the mixture until it registers 140°C/275°F on a sugar thermometer, the small crack stage (see page 66).

Using a teaspoon, pour a little toffee over each nut; it should set very quickly. When cold, remove all the nuts from the baking sheet, wrap separately in waxed paper, and store in an airtight container.

MAKES ABOUT 50 ALMONDS, 20 WALNUTS OR 15 BRAZILS

ALMOND ROCK

oil for greasing
400 g/14 oz lump sugar
75 ml/5 tbsp liquid glucose
100 g/4 oz blanched almonds
few drops of almond essence

Grease a Swiss roll tin. Put the sugar in a heavy-bottomed saucepan, add 250 ml/8 fl oz water and heat gently, stirring until the sugar has dissolved.

Add the glucose, bring to the boil and boil until the mixture registers 140°C/275°F on a sugar thermometer, the small crack stage (see page 66). Remove the pan from the heat.

Stir in the almonds, with essence to taste. Return the pan to the heat and boil for 2–3 minutes until golden brown. Pour on to the prepared baking tin and leave to set. Break into pieces, wrap in waxed paper and store in an airtight tin.

MAKES ABOUT 450 G/1 LB

MRS BEETON'S TIP Liquid glucose is a thick colourless liquid made up of glucose and maltose; not to be confused with powdered glucose (chemically pure glucose). When added to sugar syrups, it prevents crystallization. It is available from cake decorating shops and some chemists and will keep indefinitely if stored in a screw-top jar in a cool place (not the refrigerator). Acids, such as cream of tartar, also inhibit crystallization but do not necessarily prevent the process.

SNOWBALLS

Soft sugar sweets that melt in the mouth, snowballs hide a chocolate coating beneath a layer of coconut.

25 g/1 oz gelatine
400 g/14 oz sugar
5 ml/1 tsp vanilla essence
plain chocolate for coating
desiccated coconut for coating

Place 125 ml/4 fl oz water in a small bowl and sprinkle the gelatine on to the liquid. Stand the bowl over a saucepan of hot water and stir the gelatine until it has dissolved completely.

Put the sugar in a saucepan, add 175 ml/6 fl oz water and heat gently, stirring, until the sugar has dissolved. Bring to the boil and boil for 5 minutes.

Add the dissolved gelatine to the syrup and boil for 10 minutes more. Remove the pan from the heat, stir in the vanilla essence, then whisk until the mixture is stiff enough to roll into balls.

As soon as the mixture is cool enough to handle, roll it into 30–35 small balls. Melt the chocolate in a heatproof bowl over a saucepan of hot water (see Mrs Beeton's Tip). Spread out the coconut thickly on a baking sheet.

When the chocolate is ready, drop in one of the soft toffee balls. Make sure it is completely covered with chocolate, then lift it out on a fork. Tap the fork on the side of the bowl to remove surplus chocolate, then transfer the ball to the coconut-coated baking sheet. Shake the sheet gently to coat the snowball. Repeat until all the balls have been coated in chocolate and coconut, transferring the finished snowballs to a bak-ing sheet covered in waxed paper. Leave to set for 1 hour, then arrange in paper sweet cases.

MAKES 30 TO 35

> **MRS BEETON'S TIP** During melting, be very careful that no steam or condensation gets on to the chocolate, as the slightest drop of moisture will thicken it and make it useless for dipping the snowballs.

PEPPERMINT CREAMS

Children love making these simple sweets. The only problem is that they are seldom prepared to let them dry out for 12 hours before eating!

400 g/14 oz icing sugar, plus extra for
**   dusting**
2 egg whites
10 ml/2 tsp peppermint essence

Sift the icing sugar into a bowl. Work in the egg white and peppermint essence and mix to a moderately firm paste.

Knead well, then roll out on a board lightly dusted with icing sugar to a thick-ness of about 5 mm/¼ inch. Cut into small rounds.

Arrange the peppermint creams on bak-ing sheets covered with greaseproof paper and leave to dry for 12 hours, turning each sweet once. Store in an airtight container lined with waxed paper.

MAKES ABOUT 48

TURKISH DELIGHT

Illustrated on page 75

25 g/1 oz gelatine
400 g/14 oz sugar
1.25 ml/¼ tsp citric acid
2.5 ml/½ tsp vanilla essence
10 ml/2 tsp triple-strength rose water
few drops of pink food colouring
    (optional)
50 g/2 oz icing sugar
25 g/1 oz cornflour

Place 250 ml/8 fl oz water in a large saucepan and sprinkle the gelatine on to the liquid. Set aside until the gelatine is spongy. Add the sugar and citric acid, place the pan over gentle heat, and stir constantly until dissolved. Bring the mixture to the boil and boil for 20 minutes without stirring. Remove from the heat and allow to stand for 10 minutes.

Stir in the vanilla essence, rose water and colouring if used. Pour into a wetted 15 cm/6 inch square baking tin. Leave uncovered in a cool place for 24 hours.

Sift the icing sugar and cornflour together on to a sheet of greaseproof paper. Turn the Turkish delight on to the paper and cut into squares, using a sharp knife dipped in the icing sugar mixture. Toss well in the mixture, so that all sides are coated. Pack in airtight containers lined with waxed paper and dusted with the remaining icing sugar and cornflour.

MAKES ABOUT 500 G/18 OZ

VARIATION

TURKISH DELIGHT WITH NUTS
Add 50 g/2 oz skinned and coarsely chopped pistachios, almonds or walnuts to the mixture when adding the vanilla essence.

COCONUT ICE

Illustrated on page 75

To achieve the traditional pink and white effect, make two separate batches of coconut ice, colouring the second batch pale pink and pouring it on to the set white mixture.

oil for greasing
300 g/11 oz sugar
2.5 ml/½ tsp liquid glucose
100 g/4 oz desiccated coconut
few drops of pink food colouring

Thoroughly grease a 15 cm/6 inch square baking tin. Put the sugar into a saucepan, add 125 ml/4 fl oz water and heat gently, stirring until all the sugar has dissolved.

Add the glucose, bring to the boil and boil until the mixture registers 115°C/235°F on a sugar thermometer, the soft ball stage (see page 66). Remove the pan from the heat and add the coconut. Stir as little as possible, but shake the pan to mix the syrup and coconut.

Pour the mixture quickly into the prepared tin and leave to set. Do not scrape any mixture left in the saucepan into the tin, as it will be sugary. Top with a layer of pink coconut ice as suggested in the introduction, if liked.

MAKES ABOUT 400 G/14 OZ OF EACH COLOUR

> **MRS BEETON'S TIP** It is advisable to make two separate quantities of coconut ice, rather than to add colouring to half the first mixture, as the extra stirring will make the mixture grainy. Add the pink food colouring to the second batch just before it reaches the soft ball stage.

NOUGAT

Illustrated on page 75

50 g/2 oz blanched almonds, chopped
225 g/8 oz icing sugar
5 ml/1 tsp liquid glucose
50 g/2 oz honey
1 egg white
25 g/1 oz glacé cherries, chopped

Line the sides and base of a 15 × 10 cm/ 6 × 4 inch baking tin with rice paper. Spread out the almonds on a baking sheet and brown them lightly under a preheated grill. Watch them carefully; they will soon scorch if left. Whisk the egg white in a heatproof bowl until stiff.

Combine the sugar, glucose, honey and 30 ml/2 tbsp water in a small saucepan. Stir over very low heat until melted; boil to 140°C/275°F, the small crack stage. This takes only a few minutes. Remove from the heat. Whisking all the time, trickle the syrup into the egg white and continue whisking until the mixture is very glossy and beginning to stiffen.

Stir in the almond and cherries. Turn the mixture into the prepared tin and press it down well. Cover with a single layer of rice paper. Place a light, even weight on top and leave until quite cold. Cut into oblong pieces or squares and wrap in waxed paper. Store in an airtight container.

MAKES ABOUT 200 G/7 OZ

MARSHMALLOWS

400 g/14 oz sugar
15 ml/1 tbsp golden syrup
30 ml/2 tbsp gelatine
2 egg whites
2.5 ml/½ tsp vanilla or lemon essence
pink food colouring (optional)
50 g/2 oz icing sugar
25 g/1 oz cornflour

Line a 20 cm/8 inch square baking tin with greaseproof paper and brush with oil. Combine the sugar and golden syrup in a saucepan, add 125 ml/4 fl oz water and heat gently, stirring, until the sugar has dissolved. Bring to the boil and boil until the mixture registers 120°C/250°F on a sugar thermometer, the hard ball stage (see page 66).

Meanwhile, place 125 ml/4 fl oz water in a small bowl and sprinkle the gelatine on to the liquid. Stand the bowl over a saucepan of hot water and stir until dissolved.

When the syrup is ready, remove the pan from the heat and stir in the dissolved gelatine. Whisk the egg whites in a large, grease-free bowl until stiff. Pour on the syrup in a steady stream, whisking constantly. Add the flavouring and colouring, if used. Continue to whisk the mixture until it is thick and foamy. Pour into the prepared tin and leave for 24 hours.

Remove from the tin and cut into squares. Mix the icing sugar and cornflour together in a bowl and roll each piece of marshmallow thoroughly in the mixture. Leave in a single layer on a dry baking sheet at room temperature for 24 hours, then pack and store in boxes lined with waxed paper.

MAKES 40 TO 44

MINT HUMBUGS

Illustrated on page 74

oil for greasing
400 g/14 oz sugar
75 ml/5 tbsp liquid glucose
2.5 ml/½ tsp cream of tartar
2.5 ml/½ tsp oil of peppermint or to taste
few drops of green food colouring

Combine the sugar and glucose in a saucepan. Add 250 ml/8 fl oz water and heat gently, stirring until all the sugar has dissolved. Add the cream of tartar, bring to the boil and boil until the mixture registers 140°C/275°F on a sugar thermometer, the small crack stage (see page 66).

Remove the pan from the heat and add peppermint oil to taste. Pour on to a lightly oiled slab or large plate. Divide into two portions, adding green colouring to one portion.

Allow the mixture to cool until workable, then pull each portion separately as described on page 77. Using oiled scissors, cut into 1 cm/½ inch pieces, turning the rope at each cut. When cold and hard, wrap the humbugs individually in waxed paper and store in an airtight tin.

MAKES ABOUT 375 G/13 OZ

> **MRS BEETON'S TIP** An old-fashioned spill or cone, brought up to date by using modern textured paper in a bold design, is an attractive way of presenting sweets like these. If the sweets are to be a present for a child, use the cartoon section of a Sunday newspaper, backing it with thin card or construction paper for extra strength.

◇

FRUIT DROPS

If you like the idea of stocking your pantry with a supply of these sweets, for the family, as gifts and donations to bazaars, it may be worthwhile investing in a set of old-fashioned metal sweet rings, if you can find them. Otherwise, make the mixture in a baking tin and break into squares.

fat for greasing
200 g/7 oz sugar
10 ml/2 tsp liquid glucose
pinch of cream of tartar
flavourings and colourings

If using sweet rings, grease them thoroughly and place on a greased baking sheet. Alternatively, grease a 15 cm/6 inch square baking tin.

Combine the sugar and glucose in a saucepan, add 50 ml/2 fl oz water and heat gently, stirring until the sugar has dissolved. Add the cream of tartar, bring to the boil and boil until the mixture registers 120°C/250°F on a sugar thermometer, the hard ball stage (see page 66). Remove from the heat and allow to cool for 5 minutes.

Add the flavouring and colouring. Stir the syrup with a wooden spoon, pressing a little syrup against the sides of the saucepan to give it a grainy appearance.

Pour the syrup at once into the rings or in a 1 cm/½ inch layer in the prepared baking tin. Mark at once into squares and break into pieces when cold.

MAKES ABOUT 200 G/7 OZ

FLAVOURINGS AND COLOURINGS

Marry lemon flavouring with pale yellow or green colouring; raspberry or strawberry flavouring with pale pink colouring; pineapple flavouring with yellow colouring and tangerine flavouring with orange colouring.

*F*RIANDISE

oil for greasing
8 cherries
8 grapes
8 small strawberries
8 cherries
1 satsuma, in segments
8 Brazil nuts
200 g/7 oz granulated sugar

Prepare the fruit, leaving the stems on the cherries, grapes, strawberries and cherries. Remove any pith from the satsuma segments. Generously grease a large baking sheet and have ready 2 oiled forks.

Put the sugar in a heavy-bottomed saucepan and add 175 ml/6 fl oz water. Heat gently, stirring until the sugar has dissolved. Increase the heat and boil the syrup until it turns a pale gold in colour. Immediately remove the pan from the heat and dip the bottom of the pan in cold water to prevent the syrup from darkening any further.

Spear a fruit or nut on a fork, dip it in the hot caramel syrup, then allow the excess caramel to drip back into the pan. Use the second fork to ease the fruit or nut on to the baking sheet. Continue until all the fruits and nuts have been glazed, warming the syrup gently if it becomes too thick to use.

When the coating on all the fruits and nuts has hardened, lift them carefully off the baking sheet. Serve in paper sweet cases.

MAKES ABOUT 48

*R*UM TRUFFLES

50 g/2 oz nibbed almonds
150 g/5 oz plain chocolate, in squares
150 g/5 oz ground almonds
30 ml/2 tbsp double cream
75 g/3 oz caster sugar
15 ml/1 tbsp rum
grated chocolate or chocolate vermicelli
    for coating

Spread out the almonds on a baking sheet and toast them lightly under a pre-heated grill. Bring a saucepan of water to the boil.

Put the chocolate in a heatproof bowl that will fit over the pan of water. When the water boils, remove the pan from the heat, set the bowl over the water and leave until the chocolate has melted.

Remove the bowl from the pan and stir in the toasted almonds, ground almonds, cream, sugar and rum. Mix to a stiff paste.

Roll the paste into small balls and toss at once in grated chocolate or chocolate vermicelli. Serve in sweet paper cases.

MAKES ABOUT 15

MARZIPAN FRUITS AND DAINTIES

200 g/7 oz granulated sugar
5 ml/1 tsp liquid glucose
150 g/5 oz ground almonds
1 egg white
5 ml/1 tsp lemon juice
5 ml/1 tsp almond essence
icing sugar for dusting
food colouring as appropriate

Put the sugar in a heavy-bottomed saucepan and add 90 ml/6 tbsp water. Heat gently until the sugar has dissolved, then stir in the glucose. Bring the syrup to the boil and boil, without stirring, until the syrup registers 115°C/235°F on a sugar thermometer, the soft ball stage (see page 66). Remove the saucepan from the heat and immediately dip the bottom of the pan in a bowl of cold water for a few seconds, to prevent the temperature of the syrup from rising any further. Stir in the ground almonds, then the unbeaten egg white.

Return to the pan to low heat and cook for 3 minutes, stirring occasionally. Add the lemon juice and almond essence. Turn the mixture on to a board dusted with icing sugar and stir with a wooden spoon in a figure of eight movement, until the mixture is stiff, and cool enough to be kneaded with the hands. Knead in food colouring as desired, then knead in a little icing sugar until the marzipan is smooth.

If not required immediately, wrap the marzipan in waxed paper, overwrap in a polythene bag and store in a lidded container.

MAKES ABOUT 350 G/12 OZ

MARZIPAN APPLES Tint the marzipan pale green. Divide it into small pieces and shape each into a ball. Paint a little red food colouring on one side of each apple for rosiness. Make a leaf from green marzipan and use a clove as a stalk.

MARZIPAN BANANAS Tint the marzipan yellow. Divide it into small pieces and shape each piece into a roll, curving it to a banana shape. Brush cocoa powder on for shading and stick a clove into one end.

MARZIPAN LEMONS Tint the marzipan yellow. Divide it into small pieces and shape each into an oval, pointed at both ends. Roll lightly on a grater to give an authentic appearance.

MARZIPAN ORANGES Tint the marzipan orange. Divide into small pieces and roll each into a ball. Roll on a grater as for lemons and then toss in icing sugar. Press a clove into the top of each orange.

MARZIPAN STRAWBERRIES Add red food colouring to the marzipan. Divide into small pieces and shape each as a strawberry. Roll each strawberry lightly on a grater to make indentations. Top with a stalk made from a stem of angelica.

MARZIPAN CARROTS Add orange food colouring to the marzipan and shape small pieces into rolls, tapering them at one end. Make uneven indentations with the point of a knife, and press a small piece of angelica into the top as a stalk. Dust with drinking chocolate powder.

MARZIPAN PEAS Tint the marzipan green. Roll out a small piece and shape to a pea pod. Make tiny balls of green marzipan and arrange in a row in the pod. Shape a piece of marzipan to make a stalk. Place at the closed end of the pod.

MARZIPAN POTATOES Use plain marzipan, rolling small pieces into oval shapes. Mark some eyes with a skewer and dust with drinking chocolate powder.

FONDANT FOR SWEET-MAKING

A solution of sugar, liquid glucose and water boiled to the soft ball stage, fondant is used to make soft creamy sweets or chocolate centres. It can be coloured or flavoured as desired and any leftover fondant may be stored in an airtight jar.

300 g/11 oz caster or lump sugar
5 ml/1 tsp liquid glucose

Put the sugar in a heavy-bottomed saucepan which is absolutely free from grease. Add 125 ml/4 fl oz water and heat gently until the sugar has completely dissolved. Stir very occasionally and use a wet pastry brush to wipe away any crystals that form on the sides of the pan. When the sugar has dissolved add the liquid glucose and boil without stirring until the mixture registers 115°C/235°F on a sugar thermometer, the soft ball stage (see page 66). Keep the sides of the pan clean by brushing with the wet brush when necessary. Remove from the heat and allow the bubbles in the mixture to subside.

Pour the mixture slowly into the middle of a wetted marble slab or large meat dish. Cool slightly. Work the sides to the middle with a scraper or palette knife to make a smaller mass.

With a wooden spatula in one hand and the scraper in the other, make a figure of eight with the spatula, keeping the mixture together with the scraper. Work until the mass is dry and white. Gather into a ball, cover with a damp cloth and leave to rest for about 30 minutes until the fondant softens.

Break off small amounts and knead well, then knead all the small pieces together to form a ball. Store in a screw-topped jar, or wrap closely in several layers of polythene. When required, dilute with a little stock syrup (recipe follows) as required.

MAKES ABOUT 300 G/11 OZ

STOCK SYRUP

Use this syrup when diluting fondant for sweet-making or when making a pouring icing for petits fours.

150 g/5 oz granulated sugar

Put the sugar in a saucepan and add 150 ml/¼ pint water. Heat, stirring occasionally, until the sugar has dissolved, then boil without stirring for 3 minutes. Use a spoon to remove any scum that rises to the surface.

Allow the syrup to cool, then strain into a jar and cover with a lid. If not required immediately, store in a cool place (not the refrigerator) for up to 2 months.

MRS BEETON'S TIP When diluting fondant with stock syrup, work it well in, and place the bowl containing the mixture over a saucepan of hot water. Avoid overheating the mixture, however; it should only be lukewarm. The colder the fondant syrup is before being worked, the smoother the fondant will be. If worked at too high a heat, the grain will be too large and the fondant will feel and taste gritty.

FONDANT SWEETS

A fondant mat is a very useful piece of equipment for sweet making. It consists of a sheet of rubber or clear plastic about 2 cm/¾ inch deep, with fancy shapes inset, into which the liquid fondant, jelly or chocolate is poured. When set, sweets can be removed by bending back the sheet.

PEPPERMINT SOFTIES Dust a fondant mat with cornflour. Soften 300 g/11 oz fondant in a bowl over hot water. Do not overheat it. Add a few drops of peppermint essence and enough stock syrup to make a cream with the consistency of thick pouring cream. Pour into the prepared mat and leave the sweets overnight to set. Makes about 300 g/11 oz.

WALNUT FONDANTS Colour 100 g/4 oz fondant pale green and flavour with pineapple essence. Set out 36 walnut halves. Divide the fondant into 18 equal portions and roll them into balls. Flatten into pieces about the same diameter as the walnuts. Sandwich one piece of fondant between two walnut halves, pressing firmly. Allow the sweets to harden in a dry, warm place. Serve in paper sweet cases. Makes 18.

FONDANT FRUITS OR NUTS Any firm fruit that will not discolour may be used. Clean and dry the fruit, removing any stones or pips. Divide oranges or mandarins into segments. To coat 18–20 small fruits or 36–40 nuts, you will need about 200 g/7 oz fondant. Warm the fondant in a bowl over hot water, stirring it until it has the appearance of thick cream. Add some stock syrup if necessary. Dip the fruits or nuts individually in the fondant and place on a plate to dry. Cherries and grapes can be held by the stem, but other fruits and nuts must be immersed and lifted out with a fork. Take care to coat the fruits or nuts thoroughly. Use within two days.

HAND-MADE CHOCOLATES

Many of the sweets in this chapter are suitable for coating with chocolate, but the process takes time and patience. Couverture chocolate, available from supermarkets or delicatessens, should ideally be used, but must first be tempered (see below).

Alternatively, use a super-fatted commercial dipping or coating chocolate. The flavour may not be quite so good as that of couverture, but the product is much easier to use: simply break it into small pieces and melt in a bowl over a saucepan of hot water.

HOW TO TEMPER COUVERTURE CHOCOLATE Break the chocolate into pieces and put it in a bowl over a saucepan of hot water. Stirring frequently, heat to about 50°C/120°F, then allow the chocolate to cool again until it thickens (at about 28°C/82°F). Heat again to about 31°C/88°F; thin enough to use but thick enough to set quickly.

CENTRES FOR COATING

The dipping technique is described under the recipe for Snowballs on page 84.

MARZIPAN Colour and flavour marzipan, cut into attractive shapes and dip in melted chocolate.

FONDANT Colour, flavour, cut into shapes and allow to dry, then dip in melted chocolate.

GINGER OR PINEAPPLE Cut preserved ginger or glacé pineapple into small pieces, then dip in melted chocolate.

NUTS Dip blanched almonds, Brazil nuts or walnuts in melted chocolate.

CARAMELS, TOFFEE OR NOUGAT Cut into squares or rectangles and dip in melted chocolate.

COCONUT ICE Dip completely in melted chocolate or just half dip each piece.

SWEET PRESERVES

There are few areas of culinary craft more satisfying than making sweet preserves – a line of pots full of glistening jam, jelly or marmalade is reward in itself for the effort involved. You only have to sample the excellent flavour of your produce to understand why preserving is an annual treat as much as a task.

The majority of sweet preserves may be roughly grouped into two categories: those that set and those that are runny. Jams, jellies and marmalades are all set preserves, whereas conserves have a syrupy texture. Mincemeat is a combination of ingredients preserved by combining uncooked dried fruits, sugar and alcohol. It is thick rather than set. A third category, butters and cheeses, are thickened by cooking. Finally, this chapter includes fruit curd. Although this is not strictly speaking a preserve, it is used in the same way as jams and is usually regarded as a related product.

ACHIEVING A SET

Three ingredients are essential for a good set – pectin, sugar and acid. When these are correctly balanced the mixture will set.

Pectin Naturally present in some fruit, this is the glue-like ingredient found in the cell walls of the fruit. It is extracted by cooking, assisted by the presence of acid.

Sugar Sugar is added in proportion, depending on the pectin content of the fruit, then dissolved and boiled down to the right concentration for producing a set.

Acid Some fruits contain acid, others with a low acid content require the addition of lemon juice for making a good preserve. Not only does this promote pectin extraction but it also helps to give the preserve a good colour and sparkle.

INGREDIENTS

Fruit Fruit contains the maximum amount of pectin before it ripens; however in this state its flavour is not at its best. For a good preserve, the ideal is to use some fruit which is not quite ripe along with ripe fruit for flavour. Overripe fruit is not suitable for set preserves, although it may be used for butters and cheeses.

It is important to know or to check the pectin content of the fruit. Fruits with a low pectin content may be combined with others which have a high pectin content, thus ensuring that the preserve sets well.

Acid If the fruit does not have a good acid content, then this should be added in the form of lemon juice. It should be added in the initial stages of cooking to assist in pectin extraction.

Sugar Sugar should be measured carefully: too much will cause the jam to be syrupy, not set; too little and the jam will require long boiling to give a set at all, making it dark and overcooked.

Any sugar can be used; however special preserving sugar gives the best results as the large crystals dissolve slowly and evenly, producing less scum and giving a sparkling preserve. This said, granulated sugar is probably the more frequently used type and it is perfectly acceptable.

The practice of warming the sugar before

adding it to the cooked fruit helps to make it dissolve evenly and quickly.

Special sugar with pectin and acid added in the correct proportions for setting should be used according to the manufacturer's instructions. The boiling time is usually significantly shorter than with traditional ingredients. This type of sugar is very useful with low-pectin fruits or with exotic fruits.

Pectin Bottled pectin is also available for use with fruits that do not contain a good natural supply. Again, this should be used exactly according to the manufacturer's instructions.

Alternatively, fruit with a good pectin content such as apples, redcurrants and gooseberries may be cooked to a purée and used to set preserves made with fruit which does not have enough pectin. The purée is known as pectin stock. The whole, washed fruit (trimmed of bad parts, stalks and leaves) should be cooked to a pulp with water, then strained through muslin. Pectin stock may be combined with fruit such as strawberries, cherries or rhubarb to make a set preserve.

EQUIPMENT

Cooking Pan Do not use aluminium, copper, uncoated iron or zinc pans as these bare metals react with the fruit, adding unwanted deposits to the preserve and, in some cases, spoiling both colour and flavour.

A stainless steel pan is best. Alternatively, a heavy, well-coated (unchipped) enamel pan may be used. Good-quality non-stick pans are also suitable.

Although a covered pan is used for long cooking of fruit which needs tenderizing (particularly citrus fruit for marmalade), for boiling with sugar a wide, open pan is best. The wider the pan, the larger the surface area of preserve and the more efficient will be the process of evaporating unwanted liquid to achieve a set. Whatever the shape of pan, it is essential that it is large enough to hold both cooked fruit and sugar without being more than half to two-thirds full, so that the preserve does not boil over when it is brought to a full rolling boil.

Knife Use a stainless steel knife for cutting fruit. A carbon steel implement reacts with the fruit causing discoloration.

Sugar Thermometer This is invaluable for checking the temperature of the preserve.

Saucer For testing for set (not essential).

Jelly Bag and Stand For making jellies and jelly marmalades you need a jelly bag and stand to strain the cooked fruit. You also need a large bowl to collect the juice. If you do not have a stand you can improvise by tying the four corners of the jelly bag to the legs of an upturned traditional kitchen stool by means of elastic. Instead of a jelly bag a large, double-thick piece of muslin may be used. See also suggestion for straining cheese (page 28).

Jars Use sturdy, heatproof jars that are thoroughly cleaned, rinsed in hot water and dried. Unless they are exceedingly dirty or have food deposits, there is no need to sterilize jars. However they must be washed in very hot soapy water (use rubber gloves to withstand the heat), then rinsed in hot or boiling water. Turn the jars upside down on folded clean tea-towels placed on a baking sheet or in a roasting tin, then put in a warm oven about 15 minutes before use.

Alternatively, wash the jars in a dishwasher just before use and leave them undisturbed to avoid contamination. They will be hot and perfectly clean.

Jam Funnel A wide metal funnel which fits into jars and makes filling them far easier.

Small Jug For ladling the preserve into the jars.

Covers and Lids The surface of the preserve should be covered with discs or waxed paper. Airtight lids should be plastic coated as bare metal will react with fruit acids in the jam and corrode. Cellophane discs may be used with elastic bands; they are not ideal for long-term storage but are useful under lids which may not be well coated in plastic.

Labels It is important to label each pot with the type of preserve and date.

PREPARATION TECHNIQUES

All fruit should be trimmed of bad parts, stalks and leaves. Then it should be prepared according to type – peeled, cored, stoned, cut up and so on. All these trimmings including any pips, should be tied in a piece of scalded muslin and cooked with the fruit, as they contain valuable pectin.

Make sure you have enough clean and warm jars, covers and labels.

COOKING TECHNIQUES

Cooking the Fruit The prepared fruit should be cooked with acid and a little water if necessary. Soft fruits and others that yield a good volume of juice need only a little water to prevent them from drying out in the first stages of heating. The fruit must be initially cooked until it is thoroughly softened, preferably in a covered pan to prevent excessive evaporation. It is at this stage that the pectin is extracted. Undercooking not only results in tough pieces of fruit in the preserve but also in insufficient pectin for a good set.

Adding Sugar When the fruit is thoroughly cooked the sugar may be added. If possible warm the sugar first, then add it to the fruit. Keep the heat low and stir until the sugar has dissolved completely. This is important – if the preserve boils before all the sugar has dissolved, this may encourage the sugar to crystallize.

Boiling until Set Once the sugar has dissolved, the preserve should be brought to a full, or rolling, boil. This must be maintained until setting point is reached. This rapid boiling concentrates the sugar to the level needed to balance with the pectin.

Skimming At the end of cooking any scum which has collected on the surface of the preserve should be removed with a metal spoon. Sometimes a small knob of butter is added to disperse this scum or any remaining scum which cannot be removed.

Removing Stones If fruit is not stoned before cooking, the stones may be removed with a slotted spoon or small sieve as the preserve boils.

TESTING FOR SETTING

It is important to turn the heat off or take the pan off the heat when testing for setting. If the preserve continues to cook it may boil beyond the setting point, then it will not set.

Flake Test The least reliable. Lift a mixing spoon out of the preserve and allow the mixture to drip off it. When setting point is reached the preserve does not drip off cleanly but it tends to fall off, leaving small drips of flakes building up on the edge of the spoon.

Saucer Test A reliable method: have a cold saucer ready in the refrigerator, spoon a little preserve on it and set it aside in a cool place for a few minutes. Push the sample of preserve with your finger; it should have formed a distinct skin which wrinkles. If the sample does not have a skin, the preserve will not set.

Temperature Test The best test: when the correct sugar concentration is reached the boiling preserve should achieve a temperature of 105°C/220°F. Do not let the temperature go any higher.

POTTING

Before potting, warm the jars and spread clean tea-towels or paper on the surface where the jars will stand. Have ready a tea-towel to hold or steady the jars (an ovenglove is too bulky) and a dry tea-towel or absorbent kitchen paper for wiping up any bad spills on the jars. Never wipe the sides of very hot jars with a damp dish cloth or they may crack.

Most preserves should be put into jars as soon as they are cooked. The jars should be full but not overfilled. There should be just a small space below the rim of the jar to prevent the preserve from touching the lid. Cover the surface of the hot preserve immediately with a disc of waxed paper, wax-side down, then put on lids at once.

Preserves with pieces or fruit or rind which tend to float should be left to stand for 15 minutes after cooking and before potting. This allows the preserve to set just enough to hold the fruit or rind in position. The preserve should be stirred and potted, covered with waxed discs, then *left to cool completely* before covering with lids.

STORING

Store preserves in a cool, dark cupboard. They will keep from 6–12 months or longer in the right conditions. Since most modern homes have central heating, preserves tend to dry out during storage by slow evaporation. This can be averted if the rims of lids are sealed with heavy freezer tape.

BASIC FRUIT JAMS

To make a fruit jam you should know the pectin content. Fruits which have a good pectin content require an equal weight of sugar. Fruit with an excellent pectin content – currants, gooseberries or apples – can take up to 1.25/1¼ times their weight in sugar. Fruit with medium or poor pectin content will only set 0.75/¾ their weight in sugar. If the pectin content is poor, add pectin stock (see page 93), plenty of lemon juice or commercial pectin.

PECTIN TEST

Place a little methylated spirits in a clean, old jar. Add a spoonful of the thoroughly cooked fruit pulp (before sugar is added) and gently swirl the mixture. Allow the pulp to settle. If it forms a large lump, the fruit has a good pectin content. If there are a few lumps, then the fruit has a moderate pectin content. If the pulp is separated in lots of small lumps, it has little pectin and more should be added for a good set. These lumps are known as clots. Discard jar and contents after testing.

YIELD

Although it is possible to estimate the yield of most jams and many marmalades, jellies rely on the volume of juice which is extracted from the fruit for the weight of sugar which has to be added. In the recipes that follow, it has therefore not always been possible to estimate yields accurately.

APRICOT JAM

Using dried fruit and flaked almonds from the pantry, this delectable jam can be made at any time of year.

575 g/1¼ lb dried apricots
2 lemons
1.5 kg/3¼ lb sugar
50 g/2 oz flaked almonds

Wash the apricots and cut up each fruit in two or three pieces. Put them into a large bowl, cover with 1.5 litres/2¾ pints water and leave to soak for 24 hours.

Transfer the fruit and soaking liquid to a preserving pan. Squeeze the juice from the lemons. Chop one shell and tie it in scalded muslin. Add the juice and muslin bag to the apricots. Bring to the boil, lower the heat and simmer for about 30 minutes or until tender, stirring occasionally. Remove the muslin bag, squeezing it to extract all juice.

Stir in the sugar and almonds. Stir over low heat until the sugar is dissolved, then bring to the boil. Boil rapidly until setting point is reached. Remove from the heat, skim, pot, cover and label.

MAKES ABOUT 2 KG/4½ LB

APPLE AND GINGER JAM

1.5 kg/3¼ lb apples
25 g/1 oz fresh root ginger, bruised
30 ml/2 tbsp lemon juice
100 g/4 oz crystallized ginger, chopped
1.5 kg/3¼ lb sugar

Peel, core and cut up the apples, putting the peel and cores in a square of muslin with the bruised ginger. Tie the muslin to make a bag. Put the apples, muslin bag and 600 ml/1 pint water in a preserving pan with the lemon juice. Cook slowly until the fruit is pulpy.

Remove the muslin bag, squeezing it into the preserving pan. Add the crystallized ginger and sugar and stir over low heat until all the sugar has dissolved. Bring to the boil and boil rapidly until setting point is reached. Remove from the heat, skim, pot, cover and label.

MAKES ABOUT 2.5 KG/5½ LB

> 🥣 **MRS BEETON'S TIP** Central heating poses special problems when it comes to keeping jam in good condition. It is a good idea to use modern twist top jam jars which can create an airtight seal when closed immediately after potting. Seal the tops in place with freezer tape to ensure an airtight result.

Preserving Equipment

PLUM AND APPLE JAM

Illustrated on page 109

675 g/1½ lb apples
675 g/1½ lb plums
1.5 kg/3¼ lb sugar

Peel, core and slice the apples. Tie the trimmings in a piece of muslin. Wash the plums and put them into a preserving pan with the apples and the muslin bag. Add 450 ml/¾ pint water. Bring to the boil, then cook over gentle heat until the apples are pulpy and the plum skins are soft.

Add the sugar, stir over low heat until dissolved, then bring to the boil. Boil rapidly until setting point is reached. Use a slotted spoon to remove the plum stones as they rise to the surface (see Mrs Beeton's Tip). Remove from the heat, skim, pot, cover and label.

MAKES ABOUT 2.5 KG/5½ LB

> **MRS BEETON'S TIP** A stone basket, clipped to the side of the preserving pan, may be used to hold the stones while allowing the juice to drip back into the pan. A metal sieve, hooked over one side of the pan and supported by the handle on the other, performs equally well.

Testing for setting.
The saucer test

BLACKBERRY AND APPLE JAM

450 g/1 lb sour apples
1 kg/2¼ lb blackberries
1.5 kg/3¼ lb sugar

Peel, core and slice the apples. Tie the trimmings in muslin. Put the apples and muslin bag in a saucepan, add 150 ml/¼ pint water and bring to the boil. Lower the heat and simmer the fruit until it forms a pulp.

Meanwhile, pick over the blackberries, wash them gently but thoroughly and put them in a second pan. Add 150 ml/¼ pint water, bring to the boil, then lower the heat and cook until tender.

Combine the fruits, with their cooking liquid, in a preserving pan. Add the sugar and stir over low heat until dissolved. Bring to the boil and boil rapidly until setting point is reached. Remove from the heat, skim, pot, cover and label.

MAKES ABOUT 2.5 KG/5½ LB

VARIATION

SEEDLESS BLACKBERRY AND APPLE JAM Make the apple purée and cook the blackberries as described in paragraphs 1 and 2 above, then rub through a fine nylon sieve set over a bowl to remove the seeds. Mix all the fruit together and weigh the mixture. Weigh out an equal quantity of sugar. Transfer the fruit to a preserving pan and simmer until thick. Add the sugar and stir over low heat until dissolved, then bring to the boil and boil rapidly until setting point is reached. Pot as suggested above.

MORELLO CHERRY JAM

Cherries are poor in pectin and need a little help if they are to set properly. In the recipe below, commercially produced pectin is used.

1 kg/2¼ lb Morello cherries, stoned
45 ml/3 tbsp lemon juice
1.4 kg/3 lb sugar
1 (227 ml/8 fl oz) bottle pectin

Wash the cherries and put them in a preserving pan with the lemon juice. Add 200 ml/7 fl oz water. Bring to the boil, lower the heat, cover and simmer for 15 minutes.

Remove the lid, add the sugar and stir over low heat until dissolved. Bring to the boil and boil rapidly for 3 minutes. Remove from the heat again, skim if necessary and stir in the pectin thoroughly.

Cool for 15 minutes, pot and cover with waxed paper discs. Put on lids and label when cold.

MAKES ABOUT 2.25 KG/5 LB

MRS BEETON'S TIP If you make a lot of jam, it is worth investing in a good quality preserving pan. Stainless steel pans are best. Avoid iron, zinc, copper and brass pans as the fruit will react with the metal. Cooking in copper can enhance the colour of jams such as green gooseberry but the use of such pans is no longer recommended.

MARROW AND GINGER JAM

1.5 kg/3¼ lb marrow, peeled and cut up
2 lemons
100 g/4 oz crystallized ginger, cut up
1.5 kg/3¼ lb sugar

Put the marrow in a metal colander set over a saucepan of boiling water, cover the marrow with the pan lid and steam for 10–20 minutes or until tender. Drain thoroughly and mash to a pulp.

Meanwhile, grate the rind from the lemons, squeeze out the juice and place both in a small saucepan. Chop the remaining lemon shells and tie them in muslin. Add the muslin bag to the lemon mixture and pour in just enough water to cover. Bring to the boil, reduce the heat and cover the pan. Simmer for 30 minutes. Squeeze at the bag and boil the liquid, without the lid on the pan, until reduced to the original volume of lemon juice.

Combine the marrow, ginger and lemon liquid in a preserving pan. Bring to the boil, add the sugar, and stir over low heat until dissolved. Boil until setting point is reached.

Remove from the heat, skim, pot, cover and label.

MAKES ABOUT 2.5 KG/5½ LB

MRS BEETON'S TIP This jam will not produce a definite set; it is potted when it reaches the desired volume and consistency.

MULBERRY AND APPLE JAM

1 kg/2¼ lb mulberries
450 g/1 lb apples
1.5 kg/3¼ lb sugar

Pick over the mulberries, wash them gently but thoroughly and put them in a saucepan with 125 ml/4 fl oz water. Bring to the boil, lower the heat and simmer until soft. Rub through a fine nylon sieve into a bowl.

Peel, core and slice and the apples. Tie all trimmings in muslin. Put the apple slices in a preserving pan, add the muslin bag and 125 ml/4 fl oz water, then bring to the boil. Lower the heat and simmer the fruit until soft. Squeeze and discard the muslin.

Stir in the sieved mulberries and the sugar and stir over low heat until the sugar has dissolved. Bring to the boil. Boil rapidly until setting point is reached. Remove from the heat, skim, pot, cover and label.

MAKES 2.5 KG/5½ LB

RASPBERRY CONSERVE

This conserve does not set firmly but it has a wonderful fresh flavour.

1.25 kg/2¾ lb raspberries
1.5 kg/3¼ lb sugar

Put the sugar in a heatproof bowl and warm in a preheated 150°C/300°F/gas 2 oven.

Meanwhile wash the raspberries lightly but thoroughly and drain them very well.

Put them in a preserving pan without any additional water, bring them gently to the boil, then boil rapidly for 5 minutes.

Draw the preserving pan off the heat and add the warmed sugar. Return the pan to the heat and stir well until all the sugar has dissolved. Bring to the boil and boil rapidly for 1 minute.

Remove from the heat, skim quickly, pot at once and label.

MAKES ABOUT 2.5 KG/5½ LB

QUINCE JAM

This jam has a delicious flavour but is rather solid, almost like a fruit cheese.

1.5 kg/3¼ lb quinces, peeled, cored and
    cut up (see Mrs Beeton's Tip)
juice of 1 large lemon
1.5 kg/3¼ lb sugar

Combine the quinces and lemon juice in a preserving pan. Add 250 ml/8 fl oz water, bring to the boil, then lower the heat and simmer until soft.

Add the sugar, stirring over low heat until dissolved. Bring to the boil and boil quickly until setting point is reached. Remove from the heat, skim, pot, cover and label.

MAKES ABOUT 2.5 KG/5½ LB

MRS BEETON'S TIP If the quinces are very hard, they may be grated or minced coarsely, in which case the amount of water used should be doubled.

WHOLE STRAWBERRY JAM

1.5 kg/3¼ lb strawberries, hulled
juice of 1 lemon
1.5 kg/3¼ lb sugar

Combine the strawberries and lemon juice in a preserving pan. Heat gently for 10 minutes, stirring all the time, to reduce the volume. Add the sugar, stirring over low heat until it has dissolved.

Bring to the boil and boil rapidly until setting point is reached. Remove from the heat and skim. Leave the jam undisturbed to cool for about 20 minutes or until a skin forms on the surface and the fruit sinks. Stir gently to distribute the strawberries. Pot and top with waxed paper discs. Cover and label when cold. Do not use twist-top jars; the jam will have cooled down too much before potting.

MAKES ABOUT 2.5 KG/5½ LB

☀ MICROWAVE TIP Small amounts of strawberry jam can be successfully made in the microwave. The jam will have very good colour and flavour but will only be lightly set. Put 450 g/1 lb hulled strawberries in a large deep mixing bowl; the mixture rises considerably during cooking. Add 450 g/1 lb sugar and mix lightly. Cover and allow to stand overnight. Next day uncover and cook on High until setting point is reached, stirring occasionally and checking for setting every 10 minutes. Remove from the microwave, using oven gloves to protect your hands. Leave to stand, then pot as suggested above. Makes about 675 g/1½ lb.

PEACH JAM

Illustrated on page 109

1.8 kg/4 lb small firm peaches, peeled and quartered (see Mrs Beeton's Tip)
5 ml/1 tsp tartaric acid
1.5 kg/3¼ lb sugar

Combine the fruit, with the stones, and tartaric acid in a preserving pan. Add 300 ml/½ pint water, bring to the boil, lower the heat and simmer until the fruit is tender.

Add the sugar and stir over gentle heat until dissolved. Bring to the boil and boil rapidly, removing the stones as they rise to the surface (see Mrs Beeton's Tip, page 97). Test for set after about 10 minutes of rapid boiling.

When ready, remove from the heat, skim, pot, cover and label.

MAKES ABOUT 2.5 KG/5½ LB

🥣 MRS BEETON'S TIP To peel peaches, place them in a heatproof bowl, pour on boiling water to cover and leave for 30 seconds. Drain, cut a small cross in the top of each fruit and peel away the skin. Do this just before using the peaches, as they will discolour if allowed to stand.

GREENGAGE JAM

1.5 kg/3¼ lb greengages
1.5 kg/3¼ lb sugar

Remove the stalks, wash the greengages and put them into a preserving pan. Add 125 ml/4 fl oz water (see Mrs Beeton's Tip). Cook slowly for 5–20 minutes, until the fruit is broken down.

Add the sugar and stir over gentle heat until dissolved. Bring to the boil and boil rapidly, removing the stones as they rise to the surface (see Mrs Beeton's Tip, page 97). Test for set after about 10 minutes of rapid boiling.

When ready, remove from the heat, skim, pot, cover and label.

MAKES ABOUT 1.5 KG/3¼ LB

MRS BEETON'S TIP Ripe or very juicy fruit will need very little water and only a short cooking time; firmer varieties may take as long as 20 minutes to break down and will require up to 250 ml/ 8 fl oz water.

GOOSEBERRY JAM

Illustrated on page 109

1.25 kg/2¾ lb gooseberries, topped and tailed
1.5 kg/3¼ lb sugar

Put the gooseberries in a preserving pan. Add 500 ml/18 fl oz water and being to the boil. Lower the heat and simmer for 20–30 minutes, until the fruit is soft.

Add the sugar, stirring over gentle heat until dissolved. Bring to the boil and boil rapidly until setting point is reached. Test after about 10 minutes of rapid boiling. Remove from the heat, skim, pot, cover and label.

MAKES ABOUT 2.5 KG/5½ LB

DAMSON JAM

1.25 kg/2¾ lb damsons, stalks removed
1.5 kg/3¼ lb sugar
2.5 ml/½ tsp ground cloves
2.5 ml/½ tsp grated nutmeg

Put the damsons in a preserving pan with 500 ml/18 fl oz water. Place over gentle heat and cook for about 15 minutes, until the damsons are well broken down.

Add the sugar and spices and stir over gentle heat until dissolved. Bring to the boil and boil rapidly, removing the stones as they rise to the surface (see Mrs Beeton's Tip, page 97). Test for set after about 10 minutes of rapid boiling. When ready, remove from the heat, skim, pot, cover and label.

MAKES ABOUT 2.5 KG/5½ LB

MICROWAVE TIP Jam jars may be scalded in the microwave. Half fill perfectly clean jars (without metal trims) with water, place in the microwave and bring the water to the boil on High. Watch the jars closely, turning off the power as soon as the water boils. Carefully remove the jars from the microwave, protecting your hand with an oven glove or tea-towel. Pour away the water, invert the jars on a sheet of absorbent kitchen paper and leave to dry. Fill with jam while still hot.

MINT JELLY

Illustrated on page 110

1 kg/2¼ lb green apples
1 small bunch of mint
500 ml/18 fl oz distilled vinegar
sugar (see method)
20 ml/4 tsp finely chopped mint
green food colouring (optional)

Wash the apples, cut into quarters and put in a preserving pan with the small bunch of mint. Add 500 ml/18 fl oz water, bring to the boil, lower the heat and simmer until the apples are soft and pulpy. Add the vinegar, bring to the boil and boil for 5 minutes.

Strain through a scalded jelly bag and leave to drip for several hours or overnight (see page 93). Measure the juice and return it to the clean pan. Add 800 g/1¾ lb sugar for every 1 litre/1¾ pints of juice.

Heat gently, stirring until the sugar has dissolved, then boil rapidly until close to setting point. Stir in the chopped mint, with colouring, if used, and boil steadily until setting point is reached. Remove from the heat, pot and cover immediately.

PRESSURE COOKER TIP

Combine the apples and 500 ml/18 fl oz water in the pressure cooker. Bring to 10 lb pressure and cook for 5 minutes. Reduce the pressure slowly. Stir in the vinegar and boil in the open pressure cooker for 5 minutes. Mash the apples until well pulped, then strain as above and return to the clean cooker. Stir in sugar in the proportions above and add the bunch of mint, tied with string. Continue boiling until close to setting point. Remove mint bouquet and add chopped mint, with colouring, if used. Pot as above.

ORANGE SHRED AND APPLE JELLY

Illustrated on page 110

1 kg/2¼ lb crab-apples or windfalls
2 oranges
sugar (see method)

Wash the apples and cut into chunks, discarding any bruised or damaged portions. Place in a preserving pan with just enough water to cover. Bring to the boil, lower the heat and simmer for about 1 hour or until the fruit is tender. Strain through a scalded jelly bag, leaving it to drip for 1 hour.

Meanwhile wash the oranges. Squeeze and strain the juice, retaining the empty orange shells. Remove and discard the pith from each shell, then cut them in half. Put the quarters of peel into a small saucepan, add 100 ml/3½ fl oz water and cook over gentle heat for 1 hour or until tender.

Strain the water used for cooking the orange peel into a large measuring jug. Add the apple extract and the orange juice. Weigh out 800 g/1¾ lb sugar for every 1 litre/1¾ pints of liquid.

Dry the cooked peel in a clean cloth and cut into fine shreds. Set aside.

Combine the liquid and sugar in the clean preserving pan. Heat gently until the sugar has dissolved, then bring to the boil and boil fast until setting point is reached. Remove from the heat and skim quickly. Add the reserved shreds of peel; do not stir.

Leave to cool slightly until a skin forms on the surface of the jelly, then pot and top with waxed paper discs. Cover and label when cold.

CLEAR SHRED ORANGE MARMALADE

1.5 kg/3¼ lb Seville or bitter oranges
2 lemons
1 sweet orange
sugar (see method)

Wash the oranges and lemons. Squeeze the fruit and strain the juice into a large bowl. Reserve the fruit shells, pulp and pips.

Scrape all the pith from the shells and put it in a large bowl with the pulp and pips. Add 2 litres/4½ pints water and set aside. Shred the orange and lemon peel finely and add it to the bowl of juice. Stir in 2 litres/4½ pints water. Leave both mixtures to soak for 24 hours if liked.

Line a strainer with muslin and strain the liquid containing the pips into a preserving pan. Bring up the sides of the muslin and tie to make a bag containing the pith, pips and pulp. Add the bag to the pan, with the contents of the second bowl.

Bring the liquid to simmering point and simmer for 1½ hours or until the peel is tender. Remove from the heat. Squeeze the muslin bag between two plates over the pan to extract as much of the pectin-rich juice as possible (see Mrs Beeton's Tip).

Measure the liquid, return it to the pan and add 800 g/1¾ lb sugar for every 1 litre/1¾ pints of juice. Heat gently until the sugar has dissolved, then bring to the boil and boil fast until setting point is reached. Remove from the heat and skim quickly.

Leave to cool slightly until a skin forms on the surface of the marmalade, then pot and top with waxed paper discs. Cover and label when cold.

MAKES ABOUT 4 KG/9 LB

VARIATIONS

LEMON SHRED MARMALADE Wash and peel 675 g/1½ lb lemons. Shred the peel finely, removing some of the pith if thick. Cut up the fruit, reserving the pips, pith and coarse tissue. Put the fruit and shredded peel in a large bowl with 1 litre/1¾ pints water. Put the pips, pith and coarse tissue from the lemons in a second bowl and add 1 litre/1¾ pints water. Proceed as in the recipe above, boiling the marmalade rapidly in the final stages for about 20 minutes until setting point is reached.

> **MRS BEETON'S TIP** If a very clear jelly is required, do not squeeze the muslin bag; instead tie it to the handle and allow the liquid to drip slowly back into the pan.

DARK COARSE-CUT MARMALADE

Illustrated on page 110

1.5 kg/3¼ lb Seville oranges
2 lemons
3 kg/6½ lb sugar
15 ml/l tbsp black treacle

Wash the oranges and lemons. Squeeze the fruit and strain the juice into a preserving pan. Reserve the fruit shells, pulp and pips. Slice the peel into medium-thick shreds, then add it to the pan.

Scrape all the pith from the shells and tie it loosely in a muslin bag with the pulp and pips. Add to the preserving pan with 4 litres/9 pints water. Bring the liquid to simmering point and simmer for 1½–2 hours or until the peel is tender and the liquid has reduced by at least one third. Remove from the heat. Squeeze the muslin bag gently over the pan.

Add the sugar and treacle. Return to a low heat and stir until the sugar has dissolved, then bring to the boil and boil fast until setting point is reached. Remove from the heat and skim quickly.

Leave to cool slightly until a skin forms on the surface of the marmalade, then stir, pot, and top with waxed- paper discs. Cover and label when cold.

MAKES ABOUT 5 KG/11 LB

> **🍲MRS BEETON'S TIP** The quickest method of preparing fruit for marmalade is to opt for a chunky style preserve, then simply wash and chop the whole fruit, discarding pips as you work.

FIVE FRUIT MARMALADE

Illustrated on page 110

1 kg/2¼ lb fruit (1 orange, 1 grapefruit, 1 lemon, 1 large apple, 1 pear)
1.5 kg/3¼ lb sugar

Wash the citrus fruit, peel it and shred the peel finely. Scrape off the pith and chop the flesh roughly. Put the pips and pith in a bowl with 500 ml/18 fl oz water. Put the peel and chopped flesh in a second, larger bowl with 1.5 litres/2¾ pints water. Leave both mixtures to soak for 24 hours if liked.

Line a strainer with muslin and strain the liquid containing the pips into a preserving pan. Bring up the sides of the muslin and tie to make a bag containing the pith and pips. Add the bag to the pan, with the contents of the second bowl. Peel and dice the apple and pear and add to the pan.

Bring the liquid to the boil, lower the heat and simmer for 1¼ hours or until the volume is reduced by one third. Remove from the heat. Squeeze the muslin bag over the pan to extract as much of the pectin-rich juice as possible.

Return the pan to the heat, add the sugar and stir over low heat until dissolved. Bring to the boil and boil rapidly for about 30 minutes or until setting point is reached. Remove from the heat and skim quickly.

Leave to cool slightly until a skin forms on the surface of the marmalade, then stir, pot and top with waxed paper discs. Cover and label when cold.

MAKES ABOUT 2.5 KG/5½ LB

THREE FRUIT MARMALADE

One of the most popular forms of home-made marmalade, this combines the flavours of grapefruit, lemon and orange.

1 grapefruit
2 lemons
1 sweet orange

Wash the citrus fruit, peel it and shred the peel finely or coarsely as preferred. Scrape off the pith if very thick and chop the flesh roughly. Tie the pips and any pith or coarse tissue in a muslin bag. Put the peel, chopped flesh and muslin bag in a large bowl, add 2 litres/4½ pints water and soak for 24 hours.

Next day, transfer the contents of the bowl to a preserving pan. Bring the liquid to the boil, lower the heat and simmer for 1½ hours or until the peel is tender and the contents of the pan are reduced by one third. Remove from the heat. Squeeze the muslin bag over the pan to extract as much of the juice as possible.

Return the pan to the heat, add the sugar and stir over low heat until dissolved. Bring to the boil and boil rapidly until setting point is reached. Remove from the heat and skim quickly.

Leave to cool slightly until a skin forms on the surface of the marmalade, then stir, pot and top with waxed paper discs. Cover and label when cold.

MAKES ABOUT 2.5 KG/5½ LB

GRAPEFRUIT MARMALADE

1 kg/2¼ lb grapefruit
3 lemons
2 kg/4½ lb sugar

Wash the fruit and cut it in half. Squeeze it and strain the juice into a large bowl. Reserve the fruit shells, pulp and pips.

Scrape any thick pith from the shells and tie it in a muslin bag with the pips. Shred the peel finely and add it to the bowl of juice, with the muslin bag. Add 2 litres/4½ pints water and leave overnight to soften and bring out the flavour.

Next day, transfer the contents of the bowl to a preserving pan. Bring the liquid to the boil, lower the heat and simmer for 2 hours or until the peel is tender. Remove from the heat. Squeeze the muslin bag over the pan to extract all the juice.

Return the pan to the heat, add the sugar and stir until it has dissolved. Bring to the boil and boil fast until setting point is reached. Remove from the heat and skim quickly. Leave to cool slightly until a skin forms on the surface of the marmalade, then stir, pot and top with waxed paper discs. Cover and label when cold.

MAKES ABOUT 3.5 KG/8 LB

PRESSURE COOKER TIP
To adapt the recipe above, reduce the quantity of water to 1.1 litres/2 pints. Combine the juice, peel, water and muslin bag in the base of the cooker, bring to 15 lb pressure and cook for 8 minutes. Reduce the pressure quickly and remove the muslin bag. Return the open cooker to heat, add sugar and finish as above.

GRAPEFRUIT AND PINEAPPLE MARMALADE

450 g/1 lb grapefruit
1 small pineapple
juice of 1 lemon
1.5 kg/3¼ lb sugar

Wash the grapefruit, peel it and shred the peel finely. Scrape off the pith and cut up the flesh, putting the pips, coarse tissue and a little of the pith to one side. Measure the total volume of fruit and peel; it should equal 750 ml/1¼ pints. Put the flesh and peel in a bowl with 1 litre/1¾ pints water. Combine the pips, coarse tissue and pith in a second bowl and add 500 ml/18 fl oz water. Leave both mixtures to soak for 24 hours.

Next day, line a strainer with muslin and strain the liquid containing the pips into a preserving pan. Bring up the sides of the muslin and tie to make a bag containing the pith and pips. Add the bag to the pan, with the contents of the second bowl.

Cut the pineapple into slices, removing the skin, eyes and hard core; chop the flesh into small pieces. Measure the pineapple with the lemon juice; there should be 250 ml/8 fl oz. Add the mixture to the preserving pan.

Bring the liquid to the boil, lower the heat and simmer until the volume is reduced by one third. Remove from the heat; squeeze out the muslin bag. Return the pan to the heat, add the sugar and stir over low heat until dissolved. Bring to the boil and boil rapidly for about 30 minutes or until setting point is reached. Remove from the heat and skim quickly.

Leave to cool slightly until a skin forms on the surface of the marmalade, then stir, pot and top with waxed paper discs. Cover and label when cold.

MAKES ABOUT 2.5 KG/5½ LB

TANGERINE MARMALADE

Tangerine marmalade does not set readily without the addition of extra pectin.

1 kg/2¼ lb tangerines, mandarins or
    clementines
juice of 3 lemons
2 kg/4½ lb sugar
1 (227 g/8 oz) bottle pectin

Wash the fruit and put it into a preserving pan. Add 1 litre/1¾ pints water. Bring to the boil, lower the heat and simmer, covered, for 40 minutes. When cool enough to handle, remove the peel and cut up the fruit, removing the pips and coarse tissue. Return the pips and tissue to the liquid and boil hard for 5 minutes.

Meanwhile shred half the peel; discard the rest. Strain the liquid, discarding the pips and tissue, and return to the preserving pan with the fruit, shredded peel, lemon juice and sugar.

Stir over gentle heat until the sugar has dissolved, then bring to a full rolling boil. Boil hard for 3 minutes. Remove from the heat, stir in the pectin thoroughly, then return to the heat and boil for 1 minute.

Remove from the heat and skim quickly, if necessary. Leave to cool slightly until a skin forms on the surface of the marmalade, then stir, pot and top with waxed paper discs. Cover and label when cold.

MAKES ABOUT 3 KG/6½ LB

KUMQUAT CONSERVE

Illustrated on page 110

575 g/1¼ lb kumquats
1 lemon
400 g/14 oz sugar

Slice the kumquats in half and remove the pips, setting them aside. Peel the lemon, then roughly chop the flesh, setting aside the pips and any coarse tissue or pith. Tie all the trimmings in a muslin bag and put the kumquats and lemon flesh in a large saucepan. Add the muslin bag and pour in 400 ml/14 fl oz water.

Bring to the boil, lower the heat, cover the pan and simmer for 30 minutes or until the kumquats feel tender when pierced with a skewer. Squeeze out the muslin bag over the pan.

Stir the sugar into the pan, trying not to break up the fruit. Cook gently, stirring until all the sugar has dissolved, then boil until setting point is reached.

Remove from the heat and skim quickly, if necessary. Leave to cool slightly until a skin forms on the surface of the conserve, then stir, pot and top with waxed paper discs. Cover and label when cold.

MAKES ABOUT 800 G/1¾ LB

> **MRS BEETON'S TIP** Kumquats are closely related to citrus fruits; the name actually means 'gold orange'. Unlike oranges, however, they have thin edible rind and may be eaten whole. When buying kumquats, look for firm fruits with a rich aromatic smell.

PINEAPPLE CONSERVE

One large or two medium pineapples should yield enough fruit for this conserve. Cut the pineapples into slices, removing the skin, eyes and hard core, then chop into small cubes.

4 lemons
450 g/1 lb fresh pineapple cubes
450 g/1 lb sugar

Cut the lemons in half and squeeze the juice into a bowl. Cut the lemon shells into quarters and tie them in a muslin bag with the pips and pulp.

Put the pineapple cubes into a preserving pan with 60 ml/4 tbsp of the lemon juice. Add the muslin bag and 150 ml/¼ pint water. Bring the liquid to the boil, lower the heat and simmer until the pineapple cubes are tender. Remove and discard the muslin bag and use a slotted spoon to transfer the pineapple to a bowl.

Add the sugar to the preserving pan and stir over low heat until dissolved. Return the pineapple cubes to the syrup. Cook until the cubes are clear and the syrup is thick. Remove from the heat and skim quickly. Leave to cool for 5 minutes, then pot, cover and label.

MAKES ABOUT 900 G/2 LB

> **MRS BEETON'S TIP** It isn't always easy to tell whether a pineapple is ripe or not. A delicious aroma is a good guide, as is a dull solid sound when the side of the fruit is tapped with a finger. Good quality pineapples generally have small, compact crowns. Green fruit are not ripe.

SPICED APPLE BUTTER

Illustrated on page 111

3 kg/6½ lb crab-apples or windfalls
1 litre/1¾ pints cider
sugar (see method)
5 ml/1 tsp ground cloves
5 ml/1 tsp ground cinnamon

Wash the apples and cut into chunks, discarding any bruised or damaged portions. Place in a preserving pan with the cider and add 1 litre/1¾ pints water. Bring to the boil, lower the heat and simmer for about 1 hour or until the fruit is tender. Sieve into a bowl.

Weigh the pulp, return it to the clean pan and simmer until it thickens. Add three quarters of the pulp weight in sugar, with the ground spices. Stir over gentle heat until the sugar has dissolved, then boil steadily, stirring frequently, until no free liquid runs out when a small sample is cooled on a plate. Pot, cover at once, then label.

MAKES ABOUT 3.25 KG/7 LB

DAMSON CHEESE

Fruit cheeses contain a high proportion of sugar and are thus more concentrated and stiffer than other preserves. Carefully made and stored, cheeses will keep for up to two years; flavour improves with keeping.

2.75 kg/6 lb damsons
sugar (see method)
glycerine for jars

Remove the stalks and wash the fruit. Put into a heavy-bottomed saucepan or flameproof casserole (see Mrs Beeton's Tip). Add 250 ml/8 fl oz water and bring to the boil. Cover the pan, lower the heat and simmer gently for 2–3 hours or until the fruit is very tender. Drain, reserving the juice.

Have ready small clean jars without shoulders. Using perfectly clean absorbent kitchen paper, smear the inside of each jar with glycerine.

Sieve the fruit and weigh the pulp; there should be about 2.25 kg/5 lb. Put it into a preserving pan with a little of the drained juice and boil gently until very thick. Add 400 g/14 oz sugar per 450 g/1 lb fruit pulp and continue cooking, stirring all the time, until the mixture leaves the sides of the pan clean, and a spoon drawn across the base of the pan leaves a clean line.

Spoon the cheese into the prepared jars, knocking them several times on the table top while filling to force out any air holes. Cover while still hot, cool, then label.

Store for several weeks, then use like jam. For a traditional stiff cheese, store for at least a year, then turn out, slice and serve with gingerbread, butter and Cheshire or Lancashire cheese.

MAKES ABOUT 3.25 KG/7 LB

MRS BEETON'S TIP The fruit may be baked in a traditional ovenproof earthenware jar, if preferred. It will require 2–3 hours in a preheated 110°C/225°F/gas ¼ oven.

Gooseberry Jam (page 101) and Peach Jam (page 100) in the stand, with Plum and Apple Jam (page 97) in the dish

Clockwise from top left: **Mint Jelly (page 102), Kumquat Conserve (page 107), Orange Shred and Apple Jelly (page 102), Five Fruit Marmalade (page 104), Kumquat Conserve and Dark Coarse-cut Marmalade (page 104)**

Mincemeat and Lemon Curd (both on page 113), and Spiced Apple Butter (page 108)

Clockwise from plate: Piccalilli (page 126), Kiwi Fruit Chutney (page 133), Red Tomato Chutney (page 131) and Mango Chutney (page 135); serving pot contains Piccalilli

MINCEMEAT

Illustrated on page 111

200 g/7 oz cut mixed peel
200 g/7 oz seedless raisins
25 g/1 oz preserved stem ginger
200 g/7 oz cooking apples
200 g/7 oz shredded suet
200 g/7 oz sultanas
200 g/7 oz currants
200 g/7 oz soft light brown sugar
50 g/2 oz chopped blanched almonds
generous pinch each of mixed spice,
    ground ginger and ground cinnamon
grated rind and juice of 2 lemons and 1
    orange
150 ml/¼ pint brandy, sherry or rum

Mince or finely chop the peel, raisins and ginger. Peel, core and grate the apples. Combine all the ingredients in a very large bowl, cover and leave to stand for two days in a cool place, stirring occasionally (see Mrs Beeton's Tip). Pot, cover and label. Store in a cool, dry place.

MAKES ABOUT 1.8 KG/4 LB

VARIATIONS

Use a vegetarian 'suet' if you prefer a mincemeat free from animal products. If an alcohol-free mincemeat is desired, use apple juice instead of brandy and store the jars in the refrigerator if not using at once. Alternatively, freeze for up to 6 months.

> **MRS BEETON'S TIP** Observing the standing and stirring time helps to stop the mincemeat from fermenting later.

LEMON CURD

Illustrated on page 111

Lemon curd is not a true preserve but it keeps for a while in the refrigerator. Use very fresh eggs bought from a reputable source.

2 lemons
225 g/8 oz lump or granulated sugar
75 g/3 oz butter, cut up
3 eggs

Wash, dry and grate the lemons. Squeeze out the juice and put it in the top of a double saucepan or heatproof bowl set over boiling water. Stir occasionally until the sugar has dissolved. Remove from the heat and stir in the butter. Leave to cool.

Beat the eggs lightly in a bowl. Pour the cooled lemon mixture over them, mix well, then strain the mixture back into the pan or bowl. Place over gentle heat, stirring frequently until the mixture thickens enough to lightly coat the back of a wooden spoon. Pour into warmed clean jars. Cover with waxed paper discs. Put on lids and label when cold. Leave for 24 hours to thicken. Store lemon curd in the refrigerator. Use within 2–3 weeks.

MAKES ABOUT 450 G/1 LB

VARIATION

ORANGE CURD Substitute 2 oranges and add the juice of 1 lemon. Use only 50 g/2 oz butter, melting it in the double saucepan or bowl before adding the rind, juices and sugar.

BOTTLED FRUITS AND SYRUPS

Preserve the best of the summer fruits ready for very special, particularly easy, winter desserts. As well as bottled fruits to serve as the centrepiece of the sweet course, this chapter includes wonderful fruit syrups to serve with waffles, ice cream and sponge puddings.

This chapter is intended as a think-ahead dessert section. Here is a selection of preserves that may be served for the sweet course of a meal. Fruit syrups to serve with hot and cold puddings are also included.

BOTTLED FRUIT

Bottled fruits are excellent served very simply with cream or they may be served with pancakes, as a filling for a gâteau, with meringues and whipped cream or in a sponge flan. They are the superior convenience foods.

For success and food safety, it is vital to follow the timings and instructions exactly when bottling fruit. The cooking method and the timings given ensure that any bacteria present are killed. When the jars are sealed, following the instructions in this chapter, all outside moulds and other micro-organisms that could spoil the food are kept out while the fruit is stored.

Before storing bottled fruit always check that each jar is sealed. Should you discover a reject jar within a day of the fruit being processed, transfer the fruit to a covered container, chill it and use it within one or two days, as you would fresh poached fruit. If you discover that the seal on bottled fruit is gone some time after it has been stored, discard the contents in case they have been contaminated with organisms that may

cause food poisoning.

Similarly, if you find that fruit is fermenting or that it looks or tastes strange, discard it for safety's sake.

FRUIT SYRUPS

Preserve the flavour of summer fruits by making syrups that may be used for flavouring desserts. The syrups may be used to sweeten and flavour mousses, jellies, trifles or many other desserts. For the simplest of desserts, spoon a little home-made fruit syrup over good vanilla ice cream.

PREPARATION AND PROCESSING OF BOTTLED FRUIT

Bottled fruit is preserved by heating. The fruit and liquid in the jar are heated to a high enough temperature, and for sufficient time, to kill micro-organisms (bacteria, yeasts and moulds). The jar must be sealed while the contents are at the high temperature to prevent any new micro-organisms from entering.

EQUIPMENT

Preserving Jars Special preserving jars

must be used for bottled fruit. They are manufactured to withstand high temperatures and to form an airtight seal when the contents are processed correctly. The jars must be in good condition; any that are chipped, cracked or damaged in any way will not seal properly even if they do withstand the temperature during processing.

There are two types of preserving jars: screw band jars or clip jars. Screw bands, made of metal or plastic, usually have a built in rubber (or plastic) ring which provides the seal. New screw bands or sealing rings may be purchased and they should be replaced after each use. Screw bands should be loosened by a quarter turn before processing to allow for expansion when the jars are heated.

Clip jars have metal clips and separate rubber rings to seal the lids. The rubber rings should be replaced each time they are used, otherwise they will not seal the jar properly. Old, unused rubber rings should not be used as they tend to perish during prolonged storage. The metal clips expand slightly as they are heated so these jars are sealed before processing.

Saucepan and Stand The fruit may be processed in the oven or in a saucepan. The saucepan must be deep enough to submerge the jars or bottles in water. The bottles must be placed on a stand in the base of the saucepan. Slats of wood may be placed in the bottom of the saucepan or a thick pad of newspaper may be used as a stand for the jars.

Oven Method If the fruit is processed in the oven, the jars are placed on a pad of paper in a roasting tin.

Tongs, Thermometer, Oven Glove and Wooden Board Special preserving tongs are best for lifting the hot jars out of a saucepan; they are also useful for lifting jars processed in the oven. A thermometer should be used to check the temperature of the water when processing. An oven glove is essential for holding the jars and a clean, dry wooden board must be used as a stand for hot jars. Hot jars that are placed on a cold, or damp, surface will crack.

PREPARING THE JARS

The jars must be spotlessly clean. They should be washed in hot, soapy water, rinsed in hot or boiling water and allowed to drain upside down on clean tea-towels. The jars should be left upside down to drain until they are filled.

If the jars are particularly dirty (for example if they have been stored for some time) they should be sterilized. Sterilized jars should be used for any fruits that are packed in brandy or other spirit without being processed.

To sterilize jars, first wash them in hot soapy water, rinse them, then stand them on slats of wood, a rack or a pad of paper in a deep pan. Pour in cold water to completely cover the jars. Put any lids, clips and rings into the pan. Heat gently until the water boils, then boil the jars for 5 minutes. Turn the heat off and leave the jars submerged until they are to be used, when they should be drained upside down on clean tea-towels spread on a work surface.

LIQUID FOR BOTTLING

Fruit is usually bottled in syrup; however fruit juice may be used instead. The syrup may be combined with brandy or other spirits or liqueurs, or it may be flavoured with spices, such as cinnamon sticks or cloves. Strips of orange or lemon rind may also be used to flavour the syrup.

Syrup There is no rule about the quantity of sugar used in a syrup for bottling. Heavy syrups tend to make the fruit rise in the jar which spoils the appearance of the preserve (only a problem if the bottled fruit is prepared for a competition or exhibition). Brown sugar may be used if preferred but the fruit will take on the dark colour. Honey may also be used to sweeten the bottling liquid. The following is a guide to quantities of sugar to add to 1 litre/1¾ pints of water when making syrup:

light syrup   –200 g/7 oz (for apples)
medium syrup   –400–575 g/l4 oz-1¼ lb (for
                           all fruit)
heavy syrup   –800 g/1¾ lb (for peaches)

Dissolve the sugar in the water, bring to the boil and boil for 2 minutes. Remove from the heat and cover the pan to prevent any extra water from evaporating.

PREPARING THE FRUIT

Only bottle perfectly fresh, prime-quality fruit. Wash, dry and trim the fruit, then cut it into even-sized pieces if necessary. Avoid overhandling the fruit. Soft fruits, in particular, should be handled as little as possible to avoid bruising or spoiling them. Scald a wooden spoon and use its handle to ease the fruit into position when packing the jars. The fruit should be closely packed but not squashed. Apples may be solid packed, leaving little air space or room for syrup.

Apples Peel, core and cut into 5 mm/¼ inch thick slices or rings. Put into brine until all the apples are prepared to prevent discoloration. Drain and rinse well, then dry before packing. For solid packs, blanch apples in boiling water for 2 minutes, drain and pack.

Apricots Ripe, not soft, apricots may be bottled whole or halved with stones removed. Crack some stones and add a few kernels to jars of halved fruit.

Blackberries Select large, fully ripe fruit.

Cherries Select plump fruit with small stones. Morello cherries are best. Remove stalks. Stone fruit if liked, reserving all juice to add to syrup.

Currants (**Black, red or white**) Select large, ripe fruit. String and pack. Redcurrants and whitecurrants have large seeds and are best mixed with raspberries.

Damsons Remove stalks. Wipe to remove bloom. Pack whole.

Gooseberries Select green, hard and unripe fruit. Top and tail, then cut off a small slice at each end if preserving in syrup to prevent skins from shrivelling. Use a stainless steel knife to cut the fruit.

Loganberries Select firm, deep red fruit. Remove stalks and discard any fruit attacked by maggots.

Mulberries Bottle freshly picked fruit that is not overripe.

Peaches or Nectarines A free-stone variety is best so that the stones may be removed easily. Pour freshly boiling water over fruit, or plunge the fruit into a pan of boiling water, and leave for 30–60 seconds. Drain and skin. Halve the peaches and remove their stones. Work quickly as peaches discolour on standing.

Pears – cooking Firm cooking pears should be prepared as for dessert pears, then poached in medium syrup until tender. Use the cooking syrup for packing the fruit.

Pears – dessert Select fruit that is just ripe, for example Conference or William's. Peel, halve and scoop out cores with any loose fibrous flesh. Submerge prepared fruit in acidulated water (water with lemon juice added) or lemon juice until ready to pack.

Drain or rinse before packing if the flavour of the lemon juice is not required.

Pineapple Trim, peel and core. Remove all the eyes and cut the fruit into rings or cubes.

Plums Select Victoria plums that are fully grown, firm and just turning pink. Select purple varieties that are still bright red. Yellow plums should be firm and lemon-yellow in colour. Trim and wipe to remove bloom. Free-stone varieties may be halved and stoned, others should be left whole.

Raspberries Fruit must not be overripe. Pack freshly picked raspberries and avoid squashing fruit.

Rhubarb Select tender young rhubarb. Cut it into short lengths and pack. For a tight pack (not quite a solid pack), soak the prepared rhubarb in medium syrup for 8–12 hours. The rhubarb shrinks during soaking. When hard water is used for bottling rhubarb, a harmless white deposit collects on the top of the liquid. Use boiled or softened water to avoid this.

Strawberries Hull the fruit. Soak prepared strawberries in syrup as for rhubarb to shrink them before bottling.

PROCESSING METHODS

Follow these instructions very closely. When packing different fruits together, follow the highest temperature and longest processing time suggested for the types of fruit used.

QUICK DEEP PAN METHOD

1 Prepare the syrup or bottling liquid and the fruit. Pack the fruit into prepared jars and heat the syrup or bottling liquid to 60°C/140°F.

2 Have ready a saucepan deep enough to submerge the jars. Place a rack, wooden slats or a thick pad of newspaper in the bottom of the pan, then half fill it with water. Heat the water to 38°C/100°F.

3 Check the temperature of the syrup or packing liquid, making sure it is still 60°C/140°F, then pour it into the jars. Dislodge any air bubbles from between the pieces of fruit by gently shaking the jars. The jars should be just overflowing with liquid.

4 Dip rubber rings (if used) in boiling water and put them on the jars. Fix the lids with metal clips. Put on screw bands, tighten them, then undo them by a quarter turn to allow room for the jar to expand as it is heated.

5 Stand the jars in the saucepan and make sure that they are submerged in the water. The jars must not touch each other or the side of the pan.

6 Cover the pan and bring to 90°C/194°F in 20–25 minutes. Simmer for time indicated in chart on page 118. Using wooden tongs, transfer jars to a wooden surface. Tighten screw bands, if used. Clips should hold properly without attention. Leave for 24 hours.

7 Test the seal on each jar by removing the screw bands or clips and lifting the jars by their lids. If the lids stay firm they are properly sealed. Label and store.

PROCESSING TIMES FOR QUICK DEEP PAN METHOD

The following times are for jars with a maximum capacity of 1 litre/1¾ pints:

2 minutes	apple rings, blackberries, currants, gooseberries (for cooked puddings), loganberries, mulberries, raspberries, rhubarb (for cooked puddings), damsons, and strawberries
10 minutes	apricots, cherries, gooseberries (for cold desserts), whole plums, greengages, rhubarb (for cold desserts) and solid packs of soft fruit (excluding strawberries)
20 minutes	solid pack apples, nectarines, peaches, pineapples, halved plums and solid pack strawberries
40 minutes	whole tomatoes, pears
50 minutes	tomatoes (in own juice)

MODERATE OVEN METHOD

The traditional oven method processes the fruit in the oven before adding the syrup; however, the fruit tends to shrink when processed without the syrup. The following method heats the fruit in the syrup to keep shrinkage to the minimum.

1 Heat the oven to 150°C/300°F/gas 2. Fill warmed jars with the prepared fruit.

2 Pour in boiling syrup or the chosen liquid to within 2 cm/¾ inch of the top of each jar.

3 Dip rubber rings (if used) and lids in boiling water and fit them on the jars. Do not fit clips and screw bands.

4 Line a roasting tin with three or four layers of newspaper. Stand the jars 5 cm/2 inches apart on the paper.

5 Put the jars in the middle of the oven and process for the times given in the table on the right.

6 Prepare a clean, dry wooden surface on which to stand the jars. Immediately check that the necks of the jars are clean, wiping them with absorbent kitchen paper, and fit the screw bands or clips. **Do not wipe the jars with a damp cloth or they will crack.**

7 Leave for 24 hours before testing the seal by removing the screw bands or clips and lifting the jars by their lids. If the lids stay firm they are properly sealed. Label and store.

PROCESSING TIMES FOR MODERATE OVEN METHOD

Note 4 × 350 ml/12 fl oz jars require the same processing time as 2 × 700 ml/1 pint 3½ fl oz jars.

30–40 minutes (up to 2 kg/ 4½ lb) *or* 50–60 minutes (2–4.5 kg/ 4½–10 lb)	apple rings, blackberries, currants, gooseberries (for cooked puddings), loganberries, mulberries, raspberries and rhubarb
40–50 minutes (up to 2 kg/ 4½ lb) *or* 55–70 minutes (2–4.5 kg/ 4½–10 lb)	apricots, cherries, damsons, gooseberries (for cold desserts), whole plums and rhubarb (for cold desserts)
50–60 minutes (up to 2 kg/ 4½ lb) *or* 65–80 minutes (2–4.5 kg/ 4½–10lb)	solid pack apples, nectarines, peaches, pineapple and halved plums
60–70 minutes (up to 2 kg/ 4½ lb) *or* 75–90 minutes (2–4.5 kg/ 4½–10 lb)	pears

STORING BOTTLED FRUIT

Store the sealed jars or bottles in a cool, dark, dry cupboard.

APRICOTS IN BRANDY

1.8 kg/4 lb apricots
225 g/8 oz sugar
250 ml/8 fl oz brandy

You will need 3 × 450 g/1 lb preserving jars. Sterilize the jars (page 115) and drain thoroughly, then warm in an oven set at 120°C/250°F/gas ½. Wash and drain the apricots and prick them with a darning needle. Pour 300 ml/½ pint water into a large heavy-bottomed saucepan or preserving pan. Add 100 g/4 oz of the sugar; heat gently, stirring, until dissolved.

Add enough of the apricots to cover the base of the pan in a single layer. Bring the syrup back to the boil and remove the riper fruit at once. Firmer fruit should be boiled for 2 minutes, but do not let it become too soft. As the fruit is ready, transfer it to the warmed jars, using a slotted spoon.

Add the remaining sugar to the syrup in the pan, lower the temperature and stir until the sugar has dissolved. Boil the syrup, without stirring, until it registers 105°C/220°F on a sugar thermometer, the thread stage (see page 66). Remove the syrup from the heat.

Measure out 250 ml/8 fl oz of the syrup. Stir in the brandy, then pour the mixture over the apricots, covering them completely.

Process the jars following the instructions and timings given for apricots, either by the Quick Deep Pan Method or by the Moderate Oven Method. When cold, test the seals, label the jars and store for at least 1 month in a cool place before opening.

MAKES ABOUT 1.4 KG/3 LB

*F*RUIT SYRUPS

Fruit syrups may be made from overripe fruit which is not worth freezing or bottling. The juice is extracted from the fruit, then it is sweetened and processed so that it may be stored until required.

EXTRACTING THE JUICE

Cold Method This method yields the best-flavoured juice. Place the fruit in a large china or earthenware bowl and crush it with a wooden spoon. Cover the bowl and leave the fruit for 4–5 days, crushing it daily. During this standing time, the pectin which is naturally present in the fruit breaks down and the juice is released. The process may be speeded up, or tough fruits such as blackcurrants may be encouraged to soften, by adding a pectin-decomposing enzyme which may be purchased from a wine-making supplier.

Hot Method Place the fruit in a bowl over simmering water. Crush the fruit. Add 600 ml/1 pint water for each 1 kg/2¼ lb of blackcurrants or 100 ml/3½ fl oz for each 1 kg/2¼ lb blackberries. Other soft fruits do not need water. Heat the fruit gently until the juice flows easily, which will take about 1 hour for 3 kg/6½ lb fruit. Check that the water in the saucepan does not boil dry.

Straining the Juice Strain the juice through a scalded jelly bag into a large bowl. For a clear result strain the juice twice. Achieving a clear result is not essential when making syrups, so the juice may be strained through a sieve lined with scalded muslin.

SWEETENING AND PROCESSING THE JUICE

Measure the juice, pour it into a bowl and stir in 600 g/1 lb 5 oz sugar for each 1 litre/1¾ pints. Stir until the sugar dissolves – you may have to stand the bowl over a pan of simmering water.

Have ready thoroughly cleaned strong bottles with screw tops. Boil the tops for 5 minutes. Pour the syrup into the bottles, leaving 2 cm/¾ inch headspace at the top of each. Tighten the caps, then loosen them by a quarter turn. Stand the bottles on a thick pad of newspaper in a deep saucepan and pour in cold water to come up to the top of the bottles. Wedge pieces of cardboard or crumpled foil between the bottles to hold them upright.

Heat the water to 77°C/170°F and keep it at that temperature for 30 minutes. If the water is brought to 88°C/190°F it must be maintained for 20 minutes.

Have ready a clean, dry wooden board. Transfer the bottles to it and tighten their caps immediately. Allow to cool, label and store in a cool, dark, dry cupboard.

☆ **FREEZER TIP** Instead of bottling the syrup, pour it into suitable freezer containers and freeze when cold. Freezing is the easiest, and safest, storage method.

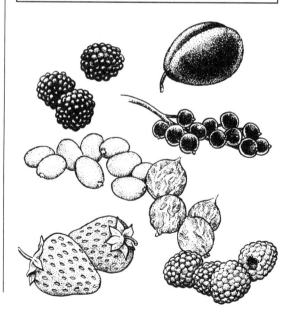

BLACKBERRY OR BLACKCURRANT SYRUP

Blackberry or blackcurrant syrups may be used to flavour mousses, ice cream, jelly or jellied desserts. This recipe produces a concentrated syrup which may be trickled in small quantities over ice creams or pancakes.

blackberries or blackcurrants
1 kg/2¼ lb crushed sugar or preserving
sugar and 15 ml/1 tbsp water for each
1 kg/2¼ lb of fruit
125 ml/4 fl oz brandy for each 1 litre/1¾
pints of syrup

Put the fruit, sugar and measured water in a large heatproof bowl. Cover with foil or a plate. Stand the bowl over a saucepan of simmering water and cook gently until the juice flows freely.

Strain the juice through a scalded jelly bag or sieve lined with scalded muslin. Measure it and pour it into a preserving pan.

Bring the juice to the boil, then lower the heat and simmer it for 20 minutes. Skim the syrup and leave to cool.

Add the brandy, then bottle the syrup, leaving 2 cm/¾ inch headspace.

Put lids on the bottles and process the syrup following the method left. Tighten the lids at once, then cool, label and store the syrup.

APRICOT SYRUP

Apricot syrup makes an unusual dessert sauce to go with pancakes, waffles or fruit fritters as well as with ice cream. Whip a little of the syrup with double cream and use to fill profiteroles or meringues.

sound ripe apricots
800 g/1¾ lb lump sugar, crushed, for
each 1 litre/1¾ pints of juice

Stone and halve the apricots then put them in a large heatproof bowl. Crack half the stones and stir the kernels into the fruit.

Stand the bowl over a saucepan of water and simmer until the fruit is quite soft and the juice flows freely. Crush the fruit occasionally.

Strain the liquid through a scalded jelly bag or sieve lined with scalded muslin. Measure the juice and weigh out the sugar. Place the sugar in a saucepan and add the juice. Heat, stirring, until the sugar dissolves, then bring to the boil. Lower the heat and simmer for 10 minutes.

Skim the syrup and pour it into warmed, clean, dry bottles. Leave 2 cm/¾ inch headspace and process the syrup following the instructions on page 120. Tighten the caps, label and store.

VARIATIONS

Substitute cherries, greengages, peaches, plums or rhubarb for apricots.

FIG SYRUP

A rich syrup to complement tangy fruit desserts: trickle a little over fresh orange segments and serve them as a topping for waffles or use the syrup with fresh orange juice to flavour home-made ice cream.

3 lemons
1 kg/2¼ lb sound, ripe, fresh figs
800 g/1¾ lb lump sugar, crushed, for
each 1 litre/1¾ pints of liquid

Use a potato peeler to pare the lemon rind thinly. Squeeze out and strain the lemon juice.

Slice the figs and put them in a bowl with 2.25 litres/4 pints water. Add the lemon rind and juice. Stand the bowl over a pan of simmering water and cook gently for 3 hours. Check to make sure that the saucepan does not boil dry.

Strain the fruit through a scalded jelly bag or fine sieve lined with scalded muslin. Measure the juice carefully.

Pour the juice into a large saucepan and add the sugar. Stir until the sugar has dissolved, then bring to the boil, lower the heat and simmer for 10 minutes.

Skim the syrup and set aside until quite cold. Bottle, leaving a 2 cm/¾ inch headspace, and process as described on page 120.

CRANBERRY SYRUP

Cranberry syrup has an excellent, rich and fruity flavour with a good bright colour. Use it to pep up bought vanilla ice cream or add it to chilled custard to make an unusual fool. It also tastes good with pancakes, waffles or steamed sponge puddings.

sound ripe cranberries
800 g/1¾ lb lump sugar, crushed, for each
1 litre/1¾ pints of juice

Place the fruit in a heatproof bowl and crush it with a wooden spoon. Stand the bowl over a saucepan of simmering water. Cook gently for 2 hours. Check that the saucepan does not boil dry, adding more boiling water as necessary.

Strain the liquid through a scalded jelly bag or sieve lined with scalded muslin. Measure carefully, pour into a saucepan and add sugar in the proportion given above.

Bring to the boil, reduce the heat and cook for 15 minutes. Skim, then leave until cold.

Pour the syrup into thoroughly clean bottles, leaving 2 cm/¾ inch headspace. Process following the instructions on page 120.

VARIATIONS

Use gooseberries, raspberries or strawberries.

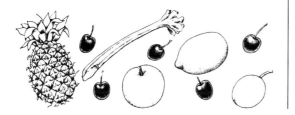

PICKLES

A selection of pickles is a prerequisite of a good pantry to complement cold meats, cheeses and home-made crackers. The selection of recipes in this chapter also includes interesting preserves to complement spiced dishes.

Vinegar is the main preserving agent used in pickles, sometimes with sugar. Since vinegar is a strong preservative, preparing pickles is comparatively easy with none of the pitfalls involved in achieving a good jam or marmalade.

PREPARING PICKLES

Vegetables should be prepared according to type, then salted for several hours or overnight. Sprinkle salt over every layer of vegetables. This extracts excess liquid and any bitter juices or very strong flavours. The salt should be rinsed off before pickling and the ingredients dried with absorbent kitchen paper. Brine solution may be used instead of salting vegetables.

Packing in Jars Thoroughly clean and dry jars must be well filled without squashing the vegetables or other ingredients.

Vinegar White or distilled vinegar, cider vinegar or white wine vinegar give pickles the best colour. Dark vinegars discolour the vegetables or fruit. The vinegar may be spiced, flavoured or sweetened as required.

Spiced vinegar may be used hot, immediately after straining, or cold. Opinions differ as to the best method but as a rule cold vinegar is always safest and should always be used for eggs and fruit whose texture may suffer from having boiling vinegar poured over them.

Pour the vinegar into the jars, shaking them gently to free any trapped air bubbles. Check the vinegar level about 24 hours after bottling the pickles, and add extra to cover the pickles if necessary.

Maturing Leave the pickles to mature for 1–3 weeks before using. Pickled eggs (hard-boiled eggs which are simply shelled and packed in jars promptly after cooking) should be left for a week; onions and other vegetables for at least 2–3 weeks.

STORING PICKLES

Cover with airtight lids, making sure that the lids do not have any exposed metal which will react with the vinegar. Label and store in a cool, dark cupboard.

Pickled eggs and fruit keep for up to 3 months. Properly stored, most vegetables keep for 6–9 months. Red cabbage should be eaten within 6 months as it tends to soften and become limp with prolonged storage.

PICKLED ONIONS

This is a recipe for onions without tears.
Soaking the unskinned onions in brine makes
them easy to peel.

450 g/1 lb salt
1.4 kg/3 lb pickling onions
2.25 litres/4 pints cold Spiced Vinegar
   (page 138)
5 ml/1 tsp mustard seeds (optional)

Dissolve half the salt in 2 litres/4½ pints
of water in a large bowl. Add the onions.
Set a plate inside the bowl to keep the
onions submerged, weighting the plate
with a jar filled with water. Do not use a can
as the salt water would corrode it. Leave for
24 hours.

Drain and skin the onions and return
them to the clean bowl. Make up a fresh
solution of brine, using the rest of the salt
and a further 2 litres/4½ pints water. Pour
it over the onions, weight as before and
leave for a further 24 hours.

Drain the onions, rinse them thoroughly
to remove excess salt, and drain again. Pack
into wide-mouthed jars. Cover with cold
spiced vinegar, adding a few mustard seeds
to each jar, if liked. Cover with vinegar-
proof lids. Label and store in a cool, dark
place. Keep for at least 1 month before
using.

MAKES ABOUT 1.4 KG/3 LB

——————— ◇ ———————

PICKLED RED CABBAGE

Do not make too much of this pickle at one time,
as it will lose its crispness if stored for longer
than two or three months.

1 firm red cabbage
100–150 g/4–5 oz salt
2–3 onions, very thinly sliced
soft dark brown sugar (see method)
600–900 ml/1–1½ pints Spiced Vinegar
   (page 138)

Remove any discoloured outer leaves
from the cabbage, cut it into quarters and
then into shreds. Layer the shreds in a
large bowl, sprinkling each layer with salt.
Cover the bowl and leave overnight. Next
day, rinse the cabbage, then drain it very
thoroughly in a colander, pressing out all
the surplus liquid.

Pack a 7.5 cm/3 inch layer of cabbage in a
large glass jar. Cover with a layer of onion
and sprinkle with 5 ml/1 tsp brown sugar.
Repeat the layers until the jar is full, using
additional jars if necessary. Fill the jar or
jars with spiced vinegar. Cover with
vinegar-proof lids. Label and store in a
cool, dark place. Keep for at least 1 week
before using.

MAKES ABOUT 1.4 KG/3 LB

PICKLED HORSERADISH

Fresh horseradish is best for cooking, but it can be hard to come by and available only in the autumn. It can be useful to keep a few jars of pickled horseradish in the larder.

horseradish roots
vinegar
salt

Wash the roots in hot water, peel off the skin, then either grate or mince them. Pack loosely in small clean jars.

Horseradish does not need to be soaked in brine, but 5 ml/1 tsp salt should be added to each 250 ml/8 fl oz vinegar used for filling the jars. Pour the salted vinegar over the horseradish to cover, close the jars with vinegar-proof lids and store in a cool, dark place.

PICKLED BEETROOT

1.4 kg/3 lb beetroot
600–750 ml/1–1¼ pints Spiced Vinegar
    (page 138)
15–20 g/½–¾ oz salt

Set the oven at 180°C/350°F/gas 4. Wash the beetroot thoroughly but gently, taking care not to break the skin. Place in a roasting tin and bake for 45–60 minutes or until tender. Cool, then skin and cube. Pour the spiced vinegar into a saucepan, add the salt and bring to the boil.

Meanwhile, pack the beetroot cubes into wide-mouthed jars. Cover with boiling vinegar and put on vinegar-proof covers. Seal, label and store in a cool, dark place for 3 months before eating.

MAKES ABOUT 1.4 KG/3 LB

MIXED PICKLE

When garden and greenhouse are bursting with new young vegetables, it is a good idea to pickle some of the surplus. For this versatile recipe any of the following can be used: small cucumbers, cauliflower, baby onions, small French beans. Only the onions need to be peeled; everything else should merely be cut into suitably sized pieces.

1 kg/2¼ lb prepared mixed vegetables
50 g/2 oz cooking salt
600–750 ml/1–1¼ pints Spiced Vinegar
    (page 138)

Put all the vegetables in a large bowl, sprinkle with the salt, cover and leave for 24 hours.

Rinse, drain thoroughly, then pack into jars. Cover with cold spiced vinegar and seal with vinegar-proof covers. Store in a cool, dark place for at least 1 month before using.

MAKES ABOUT 1 KG/2¼ LB

> **MRS BEETON'S TIP** A variety of covers are vinegar proof and thus suitable for pickles and chutneys. The most obvious choice are the twist-top or screw-on plastic-coated lids used commercially. Press-on plastic covers are also suitable. Alternatively, cut a circle of clean card or paper to the size of the top of the jar. Set it in place and cover with a piece of linen dipped in melted paraffin wax. Tie the linen firmly in place.

*B*READ AND BUTTER PICKLES

1.5 kg/3¼ lb large cucumbers
1.5 kg/3¼ lb small onions, thinly sliced
75 g/3 oz cooking salt
375 ml/13 fl oz white wine vinegar or distilled vinegar
300 g/11 oz soft light brown sugar
2.5 ml/½ tsp turmeric
2.5 ml/½ tsp ground cloves
15 ml/1 tbsp mustard seeds
2.5 ml/½ tsp celery seeds

Wash the cucumbers but do not peel them. Slice thinly. Layer with the onions and salt in a large bowl (see Mrs Beeton's Tip). Cover with a plate weighed down with a jar filled with water. Leave for 3 hours.

Rinse the vegetables thoroughly, drain and place in a large saucepan. Add the vinegar and bring to the boil. Lower the heat and simmer for 10–12 minutes or until the cucumber slices begin to soften.

Add the remaining ingredients, stirring over low heat until the sugar has dissolved. Bring to the boil, then remove from the heat. Turn the contents of the pan carefully into a large heatproof bowl. Leave until cold. Spoon into clean jars, seal with vinegar-proof covers, label and store in a cool dark place.

MAKES ABOUT 3.25 KG/7 LB

☙MRS BEETON'S TIP To make the pickle especially crisp and crunchy, cover the final layer of cucumber with about 600 ml/1 pint crushed ice before leaving the salted mixture to stand.

---

*P*ICCALILLI

Illustrated on page 112

This colourful pickle is made from a variety of vegetables. In addition to the selection below, chopped peppers (green, yellow and red), young broad beans, shallots or marrow may be used. The prepared mixed vegetables should weigh about 1 kg/2¼ lb.

450 g/1 lb green tomatoes, diced
½ small firm cauliflower, broken into florets
1 small cucumber, peeled, seeded and cubed
2 onions, roughly chopped
100 g/4 oz firm white cabbage, shredded
50 g/2 oz cooking salt
750 ml/1¼ pints vinegar
12 chillies
225 g/8 oz sugar
25 g/1 oz mustard powder
15 g/½ oz turmeric
30 ml/2 tbsp cornflour

Combine all the vegetables in a large bowl, sprinkle with the salt, cover and leave to stand for 24 hours. Rinse thoroughly, then drain well.

Heat the vinegar in a saucepan with the chillies. Boil for 2 minutes, leave to stand for 30 minutes, then strain the vinegar into a jug and allow to cool.

Combine the sugar, mustard, turmeric and cornflour in a large bowl. Mix to a paste with a little of the cooled vinegar. Bring the rest of the vinegar back to the boil in a saucepan, pour over the blended mixture, return to the pan; boil for 3 minutes.

Remove from the heat, stir in the drained vegetables, pack into clean jars and seal at once with vinegar-proof covers.

MAKES ABOUT 1 KG/2¼ LB

PICKLED GHERKINS

Small cucumbers known as dills or gherkins require longer processing than most vegetables.

25 (7.5 cm/3 inch) dill cucumbers
cooking salt
600 ml/1 pint Spiced Vinegar (page 138)
4–6 garlic cloves, peeled
4–6 dill sprigs

Select dill cucumbers/gherkins of the same size. Put them in a saucepan and cover with a solution of brine made in the proportion of 225 g/8 oz salt to 2 litres/4½ pints water.

Bring the liquid to just below boiling point, lower the temperature and simmer for 10 minutes. Drain and leave until cold, then pack into clean jars and cover with spiced vinegar. Add 1 garlic clove and 1 dill sprig to each jar. Seal with vinegar-proof covers, label and store in a cool, dark place.

MAKES ABOUT 1.4 KG/3 LB

PICKLED PEARS

10 ml/2 tsp whole cloves
10 ml/2 tsp allspice berries
5 ml/1 tsp crushed cinnamon stick
small piece of root ginger, bruised
225 g/8 oz sugar
300 ml/½ pint vinegar
1 kg/2¼ lb cooking pears

Crush the spices together and tie in a piece of muslin. Combine the sugar and vinegar in a saucepan. Add the muslin bag and heat until the sugar has dissolved.

Peel and core the pears, cut into eighths and simmer gently in the sweetened spiced vinegar until tender but not overcooked or broken. Lift out and pack in warm clean jars. Remove the muslin bag, pressing it over the pain to extract liquid.

Continue to boil the vinegar until it thickens slightly, then pour it over the pears to fill each jar. Leave until cold, then seal securely with vinegar-proof covers. Label and store in a cool, dry place for 2–3 months before use.

MAKES ABOUT 1.25 KG/2¾ LB

PICKLED NASTURTIUM SEEDS

Pickled nasturtium seeds are a good substitute for capers.

nasturtium seeds
brine in the proportion 100 g/4 oz salt to
    1 litre/1¾ pints water
Spiced Vinegar (page 138)
tarragon leaves (optional)

Gather the seeds while still green on a dry day. Steep them in a bowl of brine for 24 hours.

Set the oven at 150°C/300°F/gas 2. Drain the nasturtium seeds, rinse and drain again. Pack in small clean jars (see Mrs Beeton's Tip), place on a baking sheet and warm in the oven for 10 minutes.

Meanwhile boil enough spiced vinegar to cover the seeds. Fill the jars with vinegar, adding a few leaves of tarragon to each, if liked. Store in the refrigerator.

MRS BEETON'S TIP It is important to use small jars so that the contents can be used at once when opened.

SPICED PEACH PICKLE

2 kg/4½ lb peaches, peeled (see Mrs
    Beeton's Tip, page 100)
20 g/¾ oz whole cloves
20 g/¾ oz allspice berries
1 cinnamon stick, broken in short lengths
1 kg/2¼ lb sugar
1 litre/1¾ pints distilled vinegar

Cut the peaches in half. Remove the stones, crack a few of them and put the kernels in a small saucepan. Add water to cover, bring to the boil and blanch for 3 minutes. Drain.

Tie the spices in muslin and place with the sugar and vinegar in a preserving pan or heavy-bottomed saucepan. Heat gently to dissolve the sugar, then bring to the boil. Lower the heat, stir in the peaches, and simmer until the fruit is just tender, but not overcooked or broken.

Using a slotted spoon, transfer the peach halves to warm clean jars, adding a few of the blanched kernels to each. Continue to boil the liquid in the pan until it thickens, then remove the bag of spices and pour the liquid into the jars. Put on vinegar-proof covers while hot. When cold, label and store in a cool dark place for at least a week.

MAKES ABOUT 3.25 KG/7 LB

> **MRS BEETON'S TIP** Cinnamon is the dried bark of an evergreen tree belonging to the laurel family. Its sweet aromatic flavour is much valued in cakes, puddings, beef and lamb dishes, where the ground form is generally used. Stick cinnamon is used in pickling, making mulled drinks, in stewed fruits and to flavour sugar in the same way as a vanilla pod might be used.

PICKLED WALNUTS

One of the most delicious pickles, this, and an integral part of the Boxing Day cold table. Use green walnuts whose shells have not begun to form. Prick well with a stainless steel fork; if the shell can be felt – and it begins forming opposite the stalk, about 5 mm/¼ inch from the end – do not use the walnut.

soft green walnuts
brine in the proportion 100 g/4 oz salt to 1
    litre/1¾ pints water
Spiced Vinegar (page 138)

Place the pricked walnuts in a large bowl, cover with brine and leave to soak for about 6 days. Drain, cover with a fresh solution of brine and leave to soak for 7 days more. Drain again and spread in a single layer on greaseproof paper. Leave the walnuts exposed to the air, preferably in sunshine, for 1–2 days or until they blacken.

Pack into warm clean jars. Bring the spiced vinegar to the boil and fill the jars. When cold, put on vinegar-proof covers. Store in a cool dark place for at least 1 month before using.

> **MRS BEETON'S TIP** Always wear gloves when handling walnuts, to avoid staining.

_P_ICKLED LEMONS

No sugar goes into this pickle, so the flavour is very sharp. It is one of the few pickles that makes a good accompaniment for fish, but is very hot, so should be used with caution.

6 thick-skinned lemons
salt
750 ml-1 litre/1¼–1¾ pints vinegar
6–8 whole peppercorns
2.5 cm/1 inch piece of fresh root ginger, bruised
75–175 g/3–6 oz mustard seed
12 garlic cloves, sliced

Slit the lemons lengthways into quarters, but do not cut right through. Rub dry salt sparingly into the cuts. Put the lemons in a shallow dish, cover and leave in a cool place for 5 days or until all the salt has dissolved, turning the lemons occasionally in the liquor that forms.

Drain the lemons, reserving the liquor in a saucepan. Pack 2 lemons into each of 3 warm clean jars. Add the vinegar to the lemon liquor, with the peppercorns and ginger. Bring to the boil, skim well, then set aside to cool.

Add 25–50 g/1–2 oz mustard seeds and 4 sliced garlic cloves to each jar. Fill with the vinegar mixture, seal with vinegar-proof covers, label and store in a cool place.

MAKES 3 JARS

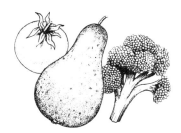

_P_ICKLED MELON OR PUMPKIN

2 large melons (honeydew or canteloupe) or 2 pumpkins
750 ml/1¼ pints white vinegar
675 g/1½ lb sugar
5 ml/1 tsp celery salt
2 long cinnamon sticks
15 ml/1 tbsp white mustard seeds
6 whole cloves
25 g/1 oz fresh root ginger, grated

Halve the melons or pumpkins and discard their seeds. Cut into wedges. Peel the wedges, then cut the flesh into small cubes. Put the cubes in a large bowl. Bring the vinegar and sugar to the boil in a saucepan, stir well and pour over the fruit. Cover and leave for 24 hours in a cool place.

Drain the melon or pumpkin cubes, reserving all the liquor and transferring it to a saucepan. Bring the liquor to the boil and add the celery salt, cinnamon, mustard seeds, cloves and ginger. Stir in the fruit cubes, lower the heat and simmer steadily for 3 hours, then pack the fruit into warm clean jars, pour on the hot vinegar and cover with vinegar-proof lids.

MAKES ABOUT 1.4 KG/3 LB

> **MRS BEETON'S TIP** White mustard seeds are not just a good flavouring; they are also a powerful preservative, which discourages the formation of moulds and bacteria in pickles and chutneys.

CHUTNEYS, KETCHUPS AND RELISHES

Chutneys, long-cooked and rich in colour are ideal for sandwiches or serving with a ploughman's lunch. Ketchups are full-flavoured preserves and relishes are ideal for adding zest to plain meats or poultry. This chapter also includes mild relishes suitable for serving with burgers or sausages; just right for summer barbecues.

PREPARING INGREDIENTS

As usual, the way in which ingredients are prepared depends on type. They should be chopped or even minced so that they eventually cook down to a thick pulp.

Peel, cores and pips should be removed. Tomatoes are best peeled but this is not necessary if they are minced or very finely chopped.

Spices Ground or whole spices may be added; usually a combination of both is used. Whole spices should be tied in a small piece of scalded muslin so that they may be removed after cooking and before potting. Cinnamon sticks are usually easy to spot in the cooked preserve, so these do not have to be tied in muslin.

Sugar Brown sugar gives chutneys a good flavour and rich colour. For lighter fruit chutneys, granulated sugar may be preferred.

COOKING CHUTNEYS

Long, slow cooking is the secret of success. A stainless steel pan is ideal (the information on saucepans to use for making sweet preserves, page 93, is also relevant to chutneys) and it must be large enough to hold all the ingredients and allow room for them to simmer steadily.

Stir the mixture occasionally until the sugar dissolves, then bring the chutney to the boil and reduce the heat so that it simmers. Cover the pan and cook for the time recommended in the recipe or until the chutney has darkened and become thick and pulpy. Stir the mixture occasionally during cooking to prevent it sticking to the bottom of the pan.

If the chutney is too liquid at the end of the recommended cooking time, or when all the ingredients are well reduced, allow it to boil, without a lid on the pan, until some of the excess liquid has evaporated. Stir frequently to prevent the mixture burning on the base of the pan.

POTTING

Have thoroughly clean, hot jars ready on a large sheet of paper or folded tea-towel. You also need a tea-towel to hold or steady the jars, a jam funnel and a small jug. The jars must have airtight lids which will not react with the metal and you should have sufficient waxed paper discs to top each preserve.

Pot the chutney as soon as it is cooked, cover with waxed paper and put on airtight lids at once. Seal the lids in place with freezer tape. If for any reason the chutney is allowed to stand before potting, lids should not be put on the jars until the preserve is cold.

STORING

Store as for other preserves, in a cool, dark cupboard. Most chutneys will keep well for up to a year.

APPLE CHUTNEY

3 kg/6½ lb apples
2 litres/3½ pints vinegar
1.5 kg/3¼ lb sugar
25 g/1 oz salt
10 ml/2 tsp ground allspice
300–400 g/11–14 oz preserved ginger,
    chopped
1 kg/2¼ lb sultanas, chopped

Peel and core the apples; chop them into small pieces. Combine the vinegar, sugar, salt and allspice in a saucepan or preserving pan. Bring to the boil, add the apples, lower the heat and simmer for 10 minutes.

Add the ginger and sultanas to the pan and simmer the mixture until fairly thick. Pour into warm clean jars and cover with vinegar-proof lids. When cool, wipe the jars, label and store in a cool dry place.

MAKES ABOUT 5 KG/11 LB

> **MRS BEETON'S TIP** Make chutney in stainless steel pans if possible. Keep a long-handled heat-resistant plastic spoon for stirring pickles and chutneys. If you prefer to use a wooden spoon, reserve one specifically for chutneys and pickles, scrubbing and drying it thoroughly after use.

RED TOMATO CHUTNEY

Illustrated on page 112

3 kg/6½ lb ripe red tomatoes
450 g/1 lb sugar
20 g/¾ oz salt
pinch of paprika
pinch of cayenne pepper
300 ml/½ pint Spiced Vinegar, made with
    white vinegar (page 138)

Peel the tomatoes (see Mrs Beeton's Tip, page 48). Immediately cut them up, removing the hard cores, and put them in a large saucepan. Add a very little water and bring slowly to the boil. Reduce the heat and simmer until thick.

Add the remaining ingredients, stirring well. Continue cooking over low heat until the mixture is thick. Test the consistency by spooning a little of the chutney on to a cold plate.

When ready, pour the chutney into warm clean jars and cover with vinegar-proof lids. When cool, wipe the jars, label and store in a cool dry place.

MAKES ABOUT 3 KG/6½ LB

> **MRS BEETON'S TIP** If this chutney is to have a good red colour, it is essential to use white sugar and white vinegar. To achieve the correct texture, the tomatoes should be processed in one continuous action from peeling to potting.

GREEN TOMATO CHUTNEY

450 g/1 lb cooking apples
450 g/1 lb onions, chopped
2 kg/4½ lb green tomatoes, roughly
    chopped
450 g/1 lb sultanas
15 g/½ oz salt
1.25 ml/¼ tsp cayenne pepper
15 ml/1 tbsp mustard seeds
1 cm/½ inch piece of fresh root ginger,
    bruised
750 ml/1¼ pints malt vinegar
450 g/1 lb demerara sugar

Peel, core and chop the apples. Put them in a large saucepan or preserving pan with the onions, tomatoes and sultanas. Stir in the salt and cayenne. Tie the mustard seeds and root ginger in a muslin bag and add to the pan with just enough of the vinegar to cover. Bring to simmering point and simmer for 20 minutes.

Meanwhile combine the remaining vinegar and the sugar in a second pan, stirring constantly over gentle heat until the sugar has dissolved. Add the vinegar mixture to the large saucepan or preserving pan and boil steadily until the chutney reaches the desired consistency. Remove the spice bag.

Pour the chutney into warm clean jars and cover with vinegar-proof lids. When cool, wipe the jars, label and store in a cool dry place.

MAKES ABOUT 3 KG/6½ LB

MRS BEETON'S TIP When filling jars, stand them on a sheet of paper to catch any drips.

YELLOW PEACH CHUTNEY

2 kg/4½ lb yellow peaches, peeled (see
    Mrs Beeton's Tip, page 100) and
    stoned
2 large onions
2 green peppers, seeded
225 g/8 oz sugar
15 ml/1 tbsp cornflour
5 ml/1 tsp salt
5 ml/1 tsp turmeric
15 ml/1 tbsp curry powder
15 ml/1 tbsp coriander seeds
7.5 ml/1½ tsp allspice berries
750 ml/1¼ pints vinegar

Mince the peaches, onions and green peppers together. In a bowl, combine the sugar, cornflour, salt, turmeric and curry powder; set aside.

Tie the coriander seeds and allspice in a muslin bag. Put the vinegar into a large saucepan or preserving pan, add the muslin bag and simmer over gentle heat for 4–5 minutes.

Remove the pan from the heat, add the sugar and spice mixture and bring to the boil, stirring frequently. Add the minced peach mixture and simmer until the chutney is thick. Remove the spice bag.

Pour into warm clean jars and cover with vinegar-proof lids. When cool, wipe the jars, label and store in a cool dry place.

MAKES ABOUT 2.5 KG/5½ LB

BANANA CHUTNEY

30 small bananas
1 small onion, sliced
25–50 g/1–2 oz chillies, chopped (see Mrs
    Beeton's Tip)
1.5 litres/2¾ pints white vinegar
225 g/8 oz seedless raisins
50 g/2 oz salt
50 g/2 oz ground ginger
450 g/1 lb soft light brown sugar

Slice the bananas into a large saucepan. Add the remaining ingredients, bring to the boil and cook over moderate heat for 2 hours, stirring occasionally. When the chutney reaches the desired consistency, pour into warm clean jars and cover with vinegar-proof lids. When cool, wipe the jars, label and store in a cool dry place.

MAKES ABOUT 3 KG/6½ LB

MRS BEETON'S TIP Leave the seeds in the chillies if you like a fiery chutney. For a milder result, remove them. Always take great care when working with chillies not to touch your lips or eyes; a strong reaction may occur on delicate skin. Wash your hands very carefully after chopping the chillies.

KIWI FRUIT CHUTNEY

Illustrated on page 112

12 kiwi fruit, peeled and chopped
2 lemons, peeled and roughly chopped
3 onions, grated
1 large banana
150 g/5 oz sultanas or raisins
100 g/4 oz preserved ginger
10 ml/2 tsp salt
5 ml/1 tsp ground ginger
225 g/8 oz brown sugar
2.5 ml/½ tsp pepper
250–300 ml/8 fl oz–½ pint vinegar

Combine the kiwi fruit, lemons and onions in a large saucepan. Slice the banana into the pan and stir in all the remaining ingredients, using just enough vinegar to cover.

Bring to simmering point and simmer gently for 1½ hours, then mash with a potato masher. Continue cooking until fairly thick, then pour into warm clean jars and cover with vinegar-proof lids. When cool, wipe the jars, label and store in a cool dry place.

MAKES ABOUT 1 KG/2¼ LB

MRS BEETON'S TIP Although kiwi fruit is now associated with New Zealand, it originated in China and was for many years known as the Chinese gooseberry. An excellent source of vitamin C, the fruit is ready to eat when it is slightly soft to the touch. Firmer kiwi fruit – often cheaper than when fully ripe – can be used for this chutney.

◈

GOOSEBERRY CHUTNEY

450 g/1 lb soft light brown sugar
1.5 litres/2¾ pints vinegar
450 g/1 lb onions, finely chopped
675 g/1½ lb seedless raisins
50 g/2 oz mustard seeds, gently bruised
50 g/2 oz ground allspice
50 g/2 oz salt
2 kg/4½ lb gooseberries, topped and
    tailed

Put the sugar in a large saucepan or preserving pan with half the vinegar. Heat gently, stirring, until the sugar dissolves, then bring to the boil and boil for a few minutes until syrupy. Add the onions, raisins, spices and salt.

Bring the remaining vinegar to the boil in a second pan, add the gooseberries, lower the heat and simmer until tender. Stir the mixture into the large saucepan or preserving pan, cooking until the mixture thickens to the desired consistency. Pour into warm clean jars and cover with vinegar-proof lids. When cool, wipe the jars, label and store in a cool dry place.

MAKES ABOUT 3 KG/6½ LB

MRS BEETON'S TIP Allspice is a berry grown in the Caribbean area. Its name derives from the flavour, which resembles a blend of cinnamon, nutmeg and cloves. It is added whole to pickles, chutneys, stews and marinades, while the ground form is used in all foods, especially cakes and puddings.

BLATJANG

Blatjang is a sweet, spicy apricot chutney from Southern Africa. It is particularly good with baked ham.

450 g/1 lb dried apricots, roughly
    chopped, soaked overnight in water to
    cover
3–4 large onions, sliced
450 g/1 lb seedless raisins, minced
450 g/1 lb soft light brown sugar
5 ml/1 tsp cayenne pepper
5 ml/1 tsp ground ginger
10 ml/2 tsp pickling spice
2 garlic cloves, crushed
1 litre/1¾ pints vinegar
50 g/2 oz ground almonds
25 g/1 oz salt

Transfer the apricots, with their soaking liquid, to a saucepan. Cook over moderate heat until soft. Put the onions in a second saucepan, add water to cover, and cook until soft.

Put the apricots and onions, with the liquid in which both were cooked, in a large saucepan or preserving pan. Add all the remaining ingredients and simmer over low heat until the mixture is smooth and firm (see Mrs Beeton's Tip). Pour into warm clean jars and cover with vinegar-proof lids. When cool, wipe the jars, label and store in a cool dry place.

MAKES ABOUT 1.5 KG/3¼ LB

MRS BEETON'S TIP To test the chutney, spoon a little on to a cold plate. As soon as the chutney is cool, tilt the plate. The chutney should not flow.

MANGO CHUTNEY

Illustrated on page 112

5 slightly under-ripe mangoes, peeled,
    stoned and sliced
25 g/1 oz salt
450 ml/¾ pint Spiced Vinegar (page 138)
5 ml/1 tsp cayenne pepper
25 g/1 oz fresh root ginger, bruised
25 g/1 oz whole black peppercorns
450 g/1 lb demerara sugar

Put the mango slices in a bowl. Sprinkle with the salt, cover and leave overnight. Next day, drain and rinse the fruit, drain it again and put it in a large saucepan or preserving pan. Add the vinegar and cayenne. Tie the ginger and peppercorns in a muslin bag and add the bag to the pan.

Bring the mixture to the boil, lower the heat and simmer for 15–20 minutes or until the mangoes are soft. Remove the spice bag and stir the sugar into the pan. Heat gently until the sugar has dissolved, then bring to the boil and boil rapidly until the chutney thickens, stirring all the time. Pour into warm clean jars and cover with vinegar-proof lids. When cool, wipe the jars, label and store in a cool dry place.

MAKES ABOUT 1.5 KG/3¼ LB

PRESSURE COOKER TIP Reduce the quantity of vinegar to 375 ml/13 fl oz. Put the mangoes in the cooker and add 250 ml/8 fl oz of the vinegar with the cayenne and spice bag. Bring to the boil, cover and cook for 5 minutes at 15 lb pressure. Reduce pressure quickly, remove the spice bag and stir in the sugar and remaining vinegar. Continue cooking in the open pan.

FRESH CORIANDER CHUTNEY

Unlike the other recipes in this section, this chutney must be served within a short time of being made. If stored in an airtight jar in the refrigerator, it will keep for up to 5 days. Serve it as an accompaniment to an Indian meal.

2 onions, finely chopped or grated
1 garlic clove, crushed
1 tomato, peeled and chopped
1 green chilli, chopped (see Mrs Beeton's
    Tip, page 133)
1 small piece of fresh root ginger, peeled
    and grated
15 ml/1 tbsp chopped fresh coriander
    leaves
45 ml/3 tbsp Tomato Ketchup (page 136)
30 ml/2 tbsp vinegar
2.5 ml/½ tsp salt
1.25 ml/¼ tsp black peppercorns

Combine all the ingredients in a bowl. Mix well. Serve at once or store in the refrigerator as suggested above.

SERVES 4 TO 5

VARIATION

For a smooth chutney, substitute 150 ml/¼ pint water for the vinegar and process in a blender or food processor.

MRS BEETON'S TIP Fresh coriander, sometimes known as Chinese parsley, is widely used in the East. Most countries use only the leaves, but the roots can be used in curry pastes, while the stalks are sometimes used for flavouring in Indian lentil and bean dishes.

WALNUT KETCHUP

Walnuts for pickling or ketchup must be picked before the shell has hardened (see page 128). In England, this usually means that picking must take place before the first week in July.

400 g/14 oz onions, chopped
2 litres/3½ pints vinegar
200 g/7 oz salt
25 g/1 oz whole peppercorns
15 g/½ oz whole allspice berries
2.5 ml/½ tsp whole cloves
1.25 ml/¼ tsp ground nutmeg
about 100 green walnuts

Combine all the ingredients except the walnuts in a large saucepan or preserving pan. Bring to the boil. Meanwhile, wearing gloves to protect your hands from staining, cut up the walnuts, crush them and put them in a large heat-proof bowl. Pour over the boiling mixture and leave for 14 days in a cool place, stirring daily.

Strain the liquid into a clean saucepan, discarding the solids in the strainer. Bring the liquid to the boil, lower the heat and simmer for about 1 hour. Bottle as for Tomato Ketchup, right.

MAKES ABOUT 1.5 LITRES/2¾ PINTS

> 🍯 **MRS BEETON'S TIP** The choice of which vinegar to use in sauce making is literally a matter of personal taste. Where keeping the true colour of the prime ingredient is important, as when making tomato ketchup, distilled white vinegar is generally used, but for other sauces malt vinegar is often preferred. Cider vinegar is particularly good with spicy fruit sauces.

TOMATO KETCHUP

Use white sugar and white vinegar to maintain the colour in this excellent ketchup.

3 kg/6½ lb ripe tomatoes, cut in quarters
30 ml/2 tbsp salt
600 ml/1 pint white vinegar
225 g/8 oz sugar
2.5 ml/½ tsp each of ground cloves, cinnamon, allspice and cayenne pepper

Put the tomatoes in a preserving pan with the salt and vinegar. Simmer until they are soft and pulpy. Rub the mixture through a fine nylon sieve or coarse muslin, then return it to the clean pan.

Stir in the sugar, place over gentle heat, and simmer the mixture until it starts to thicken. Add spices to taste, a little at a time, stirring after each addition.

Heat sufficient clean bottles to hold the ketchup; prepare vinegar-proof seals. When the ketchup reaches the desired consistency, fill the hot bottles, leaving a headspace. The ketchup will thicken on cooling, so do not reduce it too much. Seal the bottles immediately. Alternatively, allow the ketchup to cool slightly, then fill the bottles (leaving a headspace) and sterilize at 88°C/190°F for 30 minutes. Seal immediately. Label when cold.

MAKES ABOUT 1.5 LITRES/2¾ PINTS

> 🍯 **MRS BEETON'S TIP** Bottles of ketchup for keeping should be wrapped in foil. This helps to keep the colour bright.

BROWN SAUCE

1.5 kg/3¼ lb tomatoes, chopped
100 g/4 oz onions, chopped
225 g/8 oz soft light brown sugar
225 g/8 oz raisins
75–100 g/3–4 oz salt
25 g/1 oz ground ginger
1.25 ml/¼ tsp cayenne pepper
1 litre/1¾ pints malt vinegar

Combine all the ingredients in a large saucepan or preserving pan. Heat gently, stirring until the sugar has dissolved, then raise the heat slightly and cook until the tomatoes and onions are soft.

Rub the mixture through a nylon or stainless steel sieve, then return it to the clean pan. Place over gentle heat and simmer until the sauce reaches the desired consistency. Bottle as for Tomato Ketchup (left). Label when cold.

MAKES ABOUT 2 LITRES/3½ PINTS

WORCESTERSHIRE SAUCE

4 shallots, finely chopped or minced
1 litre/1¾ pints good malt vinegar
90 ml/6 tbsp Walnut Ketchup (left)
75 ml/5 tbsp anchovy essence
60 ml/4 tbsp soy sauce
2.5 ml/½ tsp cayenne pepper
salt

Combine all the ingredients in a perfectly clean bottle. Seal it tightly. Shake several times daily for about 14 days, then strain the sauce into small bottles, leaving a headspace in each. Seal tightly, label and store in a cool, dry place.

MAKES ABOUT 1.25 LITRES/2¼ PINTS

FRUIT SAUCE

450 g/1 lb cooking apples
1 lemon, peeled and roughly chopped
450 g/1 lb onions, roughly chopped
450 g/1 lb tomatoes, roughly chopped
25 g/1 oz salt
225 g/8 oz sultanas
75 g/3 oz sugar
25 g/1 oz mixed spice
1 litre/1¾ pints cider vinegar
25 g/1 oz cornflour

Combine all the ingredients except the cornflour in a large saucepan or preserving pan. Bring to the boil, lower the heat and simmer until all the fruit and vegetables are thoroughly cooked.

In a cup, blend the cornflour to a paste with a little cold water.

Sieve the cooked mixture, return it to the pan and stir in the cornflour paste. Bring to the boil and boil for 5 minutes. Bottle as for Tomato Ketchup, (page 136). Label when cold.

MAKES ABOUT 2 LITRES/3½ PINTS

CRANBERRY KETCHUP

1 kg/2¼ lb cranberries
2 onions, finely chopped
5 ml/1 tsp mustard seeds
1 cinnamon stick
1 piece of fresh root ginger, bruised
2.5 ml/½ tsp peppercorns
2 bay leaves
15 ml/1 tbsp salt
250 ml/8 fl oz white vinegar
450 g/1 lb white sugar

Put the cranberries and onions in a large saucepan or preserving pan. Add 250 ml/8 fl oz water and simmer for 20–30 minutes or until very soft.

Rub the cranberry mixture through a fine nylon sieve, then return the purée to the clean pan. Tie the spices and bay leaves in a muslin bag.

Stir the salt and vinegar into the cranberry purée, add the spice bag and simmer the mixture for 10–15 minutes, stirring occasionally.

Stir in the sugar, place over gentle heat, and simmer the mixture until it starts to thicken. Stir frequently to prevent the sauce from sticking to the base of the pan.

Heat sufficient clean bottles to hold the ketchup; prepare vinegar-proof seals. When the mixture reaches the desired consistency, discard the spice bag and fill the bottles as for Tomato Ketchup (page 136). Store in a cool, dry place for at least two weeks before using.

MAKES 1 TO 1.25 LITRES/ 1¾ TO 2¼ PINTS

SPICED VINEGAR

7 g/¼ oz each of the following spices: cloves, allspice berries, cinnamon sticks (broken into short lengths), fresh root ginger, bruised
1 litre/1¾ pints white or malt vinegar

Fold the spices in a clean cloth. Using a rolling pin, beat lightly to release the flavour. Combine the spices and vinegar in a large jug, mix well, then pour the liquid into a 1.1 litre/2 pint bottle. Seal the bottle tightly.

Shake the bottle daily for 1 month, then store in a cool dry place for at least 1 month more before straining out the spices and returning the vinegar to the clean bottle.

MAKES 1 LITRE/1¾ PINTS

RASPBERRY VINEGAR

Illustrated on page 71

raspberries
white wine vinegar
caster sugar

Clean the fruit thoroughly and measure it by volume. Put it in a bowl and add an equal quantity each of vinegar and water. Leave to stand overnight.

Next day, strain the liquid through a fine sieve or jelly bag and measure it again. To each 300 ml/½ pint liquid add 200 ml/7 fl oz caster sugar. Pour the mixture into a saucepan, bring to the boil and boil for 10 minutes. Pour the hot liquid into heated clean bottles and seal at once. Label the bottles when cold.

HORSERADISH VINEGAR

600 ml/1 pint white vinegar
50 g/2 oz grated horseradish
15 g/½ oz chopped shallot
2.5 ml/½ tsp salt
pinch of cayenne pepper
25 g/1 oz sugar

Bring the vinegar to the boil in a saucepan. Combine all the remaining ingredients in a heatproof bowl. When the vinegar boils, pour it into the bowl. Cover and set aside to cool.

Bottle the mixture and store for 10 days. It may then be used unstrained as horseradish sauce. To store the vinegar for longer than 10 days, strain it into a clean pan, bring to the boil and pour into heated bottles. Seal securely.

MAKES ABOUT 600 ML/1 PINT

STONE FRUIT VINEGAR

Illustrated on page 71

Any good quality ripe fruit with stones may be used for this vinegar. Choose from apricots, cherries, damsons, greengages, peaches or plums. Measure by volume as suggested below.

3 litres/5¼ pints fruit with stones
1 litre/1¾ pints white vinegar
800 g/1¾ lb sugar

Halve the fruit, leaving the stones in place, and put it in a large bowl. Add the vinegar, cover with a clean cloth and leave to stand in a cool place for 6 days. Stir the mixture and press down the fruit with a wooden spoon once a day. Finally press the fruit again and strain the liquid through a fine sieve or jelly bag into a saucepan.

Stir in the sugar, bring to the boil and boil steadily for 15 minutes or until the mixture is syrupy when a small quantity is tested by cooling on a plate. Skim, bottle and seal at once. Label when cold.

MAKES ABOUT 2.8 LITRES/5 PINTS

VARIATION

BRANDIED STONE FRUIT VINEGAR Allow the vinegar syrup to cool in the pan, measure its volume, then add 200 ml/7 fl oz brandy for every litre/1¾ pints. Stir, bottle and seal.

CRANBERRY VINEGAR

2 kg/4½ lb sound ripe cranberries
2.6 litres/4½ pints white wine vinegar
800 g/1¾ lb sugar for every 1 litre/1¾ pints of liquid

Put the fruit in a large, preferably earthenware, bowl. Add the vinegar, cover with a clean cloth and leave to stand in a cool place for 10 days, stirring daily. Strain the liquid through a fine sieve or jelly bag, measure its volume; pour it into a pan.

Stir in the sugar, bring to the boil and boil steadily for 10 minutes or until the mixture is syrupy when a small quantity is tested by cooling on a plate. Skim, bottle and seal at once. Label when cold.

MAKES ABOUT 3.5 LITRES/6 PINTS

VARIATION

MULBERRY VINEGAR Make as above, using 1 kg/2¼ lb ripe mulberries, 1.75 litres/3 pints vinegar and sugar in the proportion suggested. Leave for 1 week before straining.

*T*OMATO RELISH

900 g/2 lb ripe tomatoes, peeled and
    roughly chopped
450 g/1 lb cooking apples, peeled, cored
    and roughly chopped
900 g/2 lb onions, chopped
2 garlic cloves, crushed
2 green chillies, seeded and chopped (see
    Mrs Beeton's Tip, page 133)
50 g/2 oz fresh root ginger, grated
15 ml/1 tbsp paprika
15 ml/1 tbsp ground coriander
pinch of cayenne pepper
15 ml/1 tbsp salt
300 ml/½ pint white vinegar
2 bay leaves
175 g/6 oz sugar

Place all the ingredients in a large
saucepan and stir the mixture over low heat
until the sugar dissolves. Bring to the boil,
then lower the heat and cover the pan.
Simmer the relish for 20 minutes.

Uncover the pan and stir the relish, then
continue to cook at a steady simmer for
30–40 minutes more. Stir the relish
occasionally to prevent it from sticking to
the pan. When cooked the fruit and onions
should be pulpy and the relish should be
thick.

Remove and discard the bay leaves, then
pot the relish and top with waxed discs.
Cover at once with airtight lids. Label and
store for at least 3 weeks before eating.

MAKES ABOUT 1.8 KG/4 LB

*S*WEETCORN RELISH

2 green peppers, seeded and diced
2 large carrots, diced
2 large onions, chopped
6 celery sticks, diced
salt
2 garlic cloves, crushed
30 ml/2 tbsp mustard powder
5 ml/1 tsp turmeric
15 ml/1 tbsp cornflour
600 ml/1 pint white vinegar
900 g/2 lb frozen sweetcorn, thawed
100 g/4 oz sugar

Place the peppers, carrots, chopped
onion and celery in a bowl, sprinkling each
layer with a little salt. Sprinkle more salt on
top of the vegetables, cover the bowl and
leave them to stand overnight.

Next day, drain, rinse, drain again and
dry the vegetables, then place them in a
large saucepan with the garlic. In a cup,
blend the mustard, turmeric and cornflour
to a paste with a little of the vinegar. Pour
the rest of the vinegar into the pan and
bring the vegetable mixture to the boil.

Reduce the heat and cover the pan, then
simmer the mixture for 5 minutes. Add the
sweetcorn and cook, covered, for a further
5 minutes. Stir in the sugar and cook
gently, stirring, until it has dissolved.

Spoon a little of the hot liquid into the
mustard mixture, then stir the thin paste
into the relish. Add 5 ml/1 tsp salt and stir
well. Bring to the boil, stirring all the time,
then lower the heat and simmer steadily for
5 minutes without a lid on the pan. Pot and
cover at once, then label and store for at
least a week. The relish will keep for 6–9
months.

MAKES ABOUT 2.25 KG/5 LB

CRANBERRY RELISH

450 g/1 lb cranberries
450 g/1 lb cooking apples, peeled, cored
    and chopped
450 g/1 lb onions, chopped
450 g/1 lb sugar
1 cinnamon stick
6 cloves
10 allspice berries, coarsely crushed
6 juniper berries, coarsely crushed
2 blades of mace
pared rind of 1 orange
600 ml/1 pint white vinegar

Combine the cranberries, apples and onions in a large saucepan. Add the sugar. Tie all the spices and orange rind together in a square of scalded muslin and add them to the pan.

Pour in the vinegar and heat the mixture gently, stirring until the sugar has dissolved. Bring to the boil, then lower the heat and cover the pan. Cook the relish gently for 1 hour, stirring occasionally to prevent it from sticking to the base of the pan.

Remove the spices, then pot and cover the relish. Leave it to mature for at least 2 weeks before using. It keeps well for up to a year.

MAKES ABOUT 1.4 KG/3 LB

CITRUS RELISH

2 oranges
2 lemons
4 limes
1 cinnamon stick
15 ml/1 tbsp salt
900 g/2 lb onions, chopped
2 garlic cloves, crushed
300 ml/½ pint vinegar
175 g/6 oz sugar

Cut all the citrus fruit into quarters, then roughly chop each piece, discarding the pips as you work. Place the prepared fruit in a bowl, adding the cinnamon stick halfway through. Sprinkle with the salt, cover and leave for 24 hours.

Turn the fruit mixture into a large saucepan, scraping in all the juices. Stir in the onions, garlic and vinegar. Bring to the boil, then lower the heat and cover the pan. Simmer the mixture for 1 hour, stirring occasionally, or until the fruit is tender.

Discard the cinnamon stick, then stir in the sugar and cook over low heat until the sugar has dissolved, stirring all the time. Increase the heat and simmer the relish for a further 15 minutes without a lid on the pan.

Pot and cover the relish, then label and leave for at least 3 weeks for the flavour to mature.

MAKES ABOUT 1.4 KG/3 LB

INDEX